To Di
from Rosa x.

The F

o

ANNE and HELEN
CARUANA GALIZIA

PAX BOOKS
2001

First published in Malta 1999
Reprinted 2001
Published in England 1997 by Prospect Books

ISBN: 99932-0-003-4

Pax Books
75 Quentin Road, London SE13 5DG, England

e-mail: anne_parnis@picknowl.com.au
e-mail: helencgalizia@clara.co.uk

Printed by P.E.G. Ltd, San Gwann, Malta

TO THE MEMORY OF
MAY, VICTOR AND MARY CLARE,
FROM WHOM WE LEARNED MUCH
ABOUT COOKERY IN GENERAL
AND LIFE IN PARTICULAR

CONTENTS

ACKNOWLEDGEMENTS

If we had not received so much generous help from our families, friends and other cookery writers, this book would never have come into print. Sadly, many of the close relatives and friends who contributed to this work have died and we wish to record their names – May and Victor Caruana Galizia, (our parents), our sister Mary Clare Manduca (née Caruana Galizia), Agnes Asphar, Louise Caruana Galizia, Lily Arrigo (née Caruana Galizia), Mary Caruana Galizia (née Lupi), Esther Lupi, Lucy Parnis, Roger Parnis, Teresa Farrugia and Pawla Vella. Our father, Victor, never lived to see even the first publication though, prior to his death, he had begun to help and advise us. It was he who inspired us with his expertise and his enjoyment of cooking for friends and family. He found cooking an ideal form of relaxation for a tired mind and we do too, particularly when the results are enjoyed by others. Our mother, May (née Asphar), taught us the foundations of good cookery, adding a Scottish touch which she gained when she lived for some time with a family in rural Scotland in her youth. We were brought up on accounts of this memorable period of her life, the thrilling experience of picking fresh raspberries and mushrooms, learning how to churn butter and make exquisite pastry – all learned from the mother of that family who, we were told solemnly, 'had studied science'. May's knowledge of traditional Maltese cookery came, not surprisingly from her own mother and it is to them that we owe thanks for teaching us to prepare (amongst other things) our versions of *minestra* and for the addition of *fidloqqom* (borage) to the *soppa tal-armla*.

We wish to acknowledge, also, the encouragement we received from four outstanding writers, Elizabeth David, Jane Grigson (both of whom died in the 1980s), Frances Bissell and Alan Davidson, all of whom have written exquisitely and extensively about France and other European and Mediterranean countries. Such was the influence and power and pervasiveness of the British Empire that it is not surprising that after the war years when food and books once again became available, we learned as much about Mediterranean cookery from English writers as from French, Greek, Italian and North African ones. Special thanks are given to Alan Davidson who generously commented on our drafts and made immensely useful comments and corrections. And to Frances Bissell who not only introduced us to our publisher in England but was the first serious cookery writer in England to discover and publicize good Maltese and Gozitan cookery. This has given us enormous encouragement after many years during which British journalists went out of their way to draw attention only to bad examples of Maltese cuisine.

The help we were given by three of our Caruana Galizia aunts, Rosa Darmanin, Teresa Swan and Marcelle (née Mamo), as well as those mentioned above, was immeasurable. They patiently gave detailed instructions and guidance, unearthed old family recipes and answered frequent enquiries. Mary (née Lupi) gave us her excellent recipe for *torta tal-marmurat* made with home-made candied peel; Mary Clare Manduca (our eldest sister) passed on the old Asphar recipe for an exquisite tomato jam. Pawla Vella, who worked in our grandmother's family for over 50 years, helped with recipes, technicalities and important details. You will find her own recipe for Marsala cake.

We owe special thanks to Teresa Cachia Zammit who, during our frequent absences from the islands, kept us up to date with new publications which had a bearing on our work. John Manduca also kindly commented on sections of our text.

We express our thanks to Lawrence Pollinger Ltd and to the estate of the late Mrs Frieda Lawrence and to William Heinemann Ltd for permission to quote from 'Sea and Sardinia' by D.H. Lawrence.

We thank the Hon. Mrs Caroline Mieczkowska for permission to quote from private correspondence between her grandfather Lord Grenfell and Joseph Chamberlain, Colonial Secretary during the period of Lord Grenfell's governorship of Malta (1899–1903).

We would also like to thank Jacqueline Busuttil, Miriam Chetcuti, Lilian Tabone, Sylvia Manduca, Dolores Meilak, Renée Debono, Yvonne Mamo, Kelina Sultana, V. Xerri, Elizabeth Parnis, Clara Tait, Dr Mary Darmanin, Francis and Michael Darmanin, Frank Fabri, Michael Luke, Dr Ena Cremona, Mrs M. Portelli, Hugh Lillingston, Michael Calascione, Anthony Camilleri (the London Butcher at Birżebbuġa), Maria Galea (the Prime Butcher at Rabat), Mr and Mrs Emmanuel Mifsud (bakers at Birżebbuġa), Mr Franz Saliba (owner of the St Helen's Street Bakery in Sliema), G. Pace and E. Falzon (of the former Milk Marketing Undertaking), Sue Camilleri Preziosi, Ruth and Frank Williams, Tom Jaine, Jeri Wagner, and Heidi Lascelles. Anna and Guy Evans gave general guidance and Mrs Evans also granted permission to quote from the works of her father, Professor A. J. Arberry. Julian and Victor Manduca advised us on the current restaurant scene in Malta and, notwithstanding their own strict (though not flaunted) vegetarianism, helped us in a number of ways over many years and advised us on vegetarianism and endangered species. To all the above we owe a debt of thanks.

We owe special thanks to our husbands, Roger Parnis (1923–1993), and Richard Tomkins and to every one of our children for their enthusiasm, encouragement and support over many years.

MALTESE COOKING TODAY

'Then fry bacon – good English bacon from Malta, a god-send indeed.'

D. H. Lawrence

In the first version of this book, written in 1972, we wrote the following introduction:

'This should, perhaps, be entitled "In Defence of Maltese Cookery", for so much has been written and said about our cuisine (or the lack of it) by tourists, settlers and foreign journalists, that some explanation is called for. It is only recently that any demand has been made for Maltese food. We are an amenable people and very hospitable, and it has been the Maltese custom to make the foreigner feel at home, whether he is a serviceman stationed on the island or just a visitor, and to provide the food and drink which he misses while he is away from home. One has only to walk down "The Gut" to see countless restaurants offering eggs and bacon, fish and chips and tea to realize this. The larger, more expensive, restaurants have for years been supplying conventional international dishes like steak and roast chicken.

'Where, then, is the real Maltese cookery? It is going on still as it has been for hundreds of years, in Maltese homes, and any visitor who has been invited to eat with a Maltese family will vouch for its goodness. When one considers the size of the island one realizes why Malta has never been a country of restaurants. Most workers return home at lunchtime for the main meal of the day, followed by a siesta in the summer months. In the evening a light meal of eggs, salad or left-overs is prepared. The manual worker takes his lunch to the working site. This usually consists of half a loaf of our excellent bread, hollowed out and filled with tomatoes, oil, olives, anchovies or cheese, and accompanied by a glass of wine. His main meal is in the evening.

'There has not been much need for restaurants until now, though one must mention that there are a few exceptions – such as those in Valletta and the seaside resorts, long established and patronized by the Maltese and by foreigners for many years.

'Now Malta has suddenly become one of the most popular tourist centres in Europe. Tourism must be its livelihood, and tourism makes many demands on a country and its people. They are watched and observed, photographed, analysed and interviewed . . . Malta, with its long and troubled history of invasions and occupations is invaded once more – but sweetly now – by estate agents, tycoons, speculators and celebrities, and last, but not least, by thousands of holiday-makers. Malta's character is changing: its landscape defaced by many concrete hotels, blocks of flats and so-called "authentic" villas. The national food is one of the characteristics of a country which most tourists seek and Malta has failed to provide them with this, though the situation is gradually improving. A number of restaurants now attempt to provide a purely Maltese menu.

'A few books on Maltese cookery have been published but none of them is comprehensive, and we have tried in this book to include all recipes which are typically Maltese. Because of Malta's closeness to Italy, "pasta" has always been one of the staple foods of the country and we have not therefore included any recipes for Italian pasta dishes (like lasagne) as these may be found in many other books. Our recipes have been passed on from mother to daughter for generations but never committed to paper, and it has been a hard task to collect them.

'The French occupation of the island, brief though it was, left its mark. It is thought that the term *għad-dobbu* is a corruption of the French *en daube*. It is an amusing thought that the rather tasteless bread, similar to the wrapped loaf one so deplores in England, is known here as "French" bread. It is said to have originated during Napoleon's occupation when his troops refused to eat the local product and provided their own bread.

'The most recent influence is, of course, the English one – the traditional roast turkey is eaten at Christmas, followed by Christmas pudding – but often preceded by our *timpana*! Malta belonged to Britain for 150 years and it is not surprising that Maltese restaurant cooking has concentrated almost exclusively on English-inspired dishes. It will be interesting to see what will have become of Maltese cookery in, say, a hundred years time, now that the island is independent.

'We hope that this book will help to reintroduce Maltese cooking to the Maltese as well as to our visitors. No great claims can be made for our cuisine. It is essentially simple, not subtle, and its extent is limited, but the visitors who have sampled it have liked it, and we hope you will enjoy experimenting with these recipes.'

❖❖❖❖❖

MENU FOR A FAREWELL DINNER PARTY GIVEN BY A MALTESE FAMILY ON THE 23RD OF FEBRUARY 1888

We include this menu to give readers an idea of the kind of food the affluent classes considered appropriate for a celebration towards the end of Queen Victoria's reign and, in tune with those times, the menu was adorned with butterflies sticking out from the top and bottom corners. Only one course appears to be Maltese (and even that is of Neapolitan origin!)

POTAGES

à la Reine
Brunoise

ENTRÉES

Gâteau à la Napolitaine
Ris de Veau aux champignons

RELEVEÉS

Dindon rôti
Jambon
Boeuf rôti à l'Anglaise

RÔTS

Cailles à la Royale
Asperges glacées

ENTREMETS

Boudin à la Victoria
Pomme à la Napoleon

GLACE

DESSERT

Our original work "Recipes from Malta" (of which this is a revised and thoroughly updated edition) was a considerable success and in print for more than 20 years. Twenty four years later we have been encouraged to make some observations about the ways cooking and eating have changed.

There have certainly been changes for the better but the reputation of Maltese cookery still needs to be defended. The restaurant scene has improved dramatically and a number of places have incorporated Maltese dishes into their menus. Italian cooking is much more in evidence both in our homes and in a few genuinely Italian restaurants since the range of locally produced and imported foods has grown. The cuisines of various nationalities are well represented and this is a welcome development for the Maltese themselves who want to eat something other than Maltese or Italian food when they go out. Yet so many of the less expensive Maltese restaurants still excel in the art of offering British tourists, in particular, their favourite English dishes. The food offerings of The Gut are no longer, yet it seems to be a chronic case of "plus ca change . . ." The category of English visitor has changed (the British holiday maker having replaced the British serviceman) but the food which the popular tourist restaurant and cafe lures them in with is the same. "Chips with everything" is a common criticism of restaurants everywhere but, in Malta, not only do the chips themselves frequently disappoint, it is what accompanies them which can be so alarming – tough, overcooked and mushy steaks, frozen imported fish, nondescript chicken teamed up with pathetic attempts at salad, bottled salad creams and so on. One expensive seaside restaurant (which has lost all its simple charm due to re-decoration in a totally inappropriate style) has been topping its salads with nasty, bottled, pickled vegetables for the past 40 years!

There have been so many contributions to our cuisine – not a surprising fact when one considers Malta's location and its social and economic history and the successive waves of dominations. How different from large countries, like France, where cooking and eating traditions evolved amongst the indigenous people over many generations developing and perfecting their cuisines with relatively few outside influences. One could make a very wide and speculative generalisation about the sources previous to the recent British and current Italian/European ones.

Indigenous peasant food (for want of a better description) is characterised by frugality with irregular feasts of meat, game and fish when these are obtainable, always with vegetables as the main element. What people eat, anywhere, as their regular diet, is determined by their economic status – yet all over the world certain dishes are loved by rich and poor alike – in our case, minestra, for example, and ġbejniet freshly made from sheep or goats milk are highly regarded by every section of the population. Does poverty stifle culinary creativity? We believe it does. We have heard peasants remark "il fenek issajru hekk" (you cook a rabbit in this way) – and sound quite surprised at the idea of cooking rabbit in a different way. After all, if one acquired a rabbit only very occasionally it would seem unnecessary to devise a different way of cooking it every time! Variety and adventure in food preparation also stems from regional diversity but our tiny islands can scarcely uphold regional differences. It is true that Gozitan cookery does present a few variations. Yet in the past there may have been different culinary practices until the early part of this century when cars and buses began to replace horse and cart. Before that time different villages boasted different dialects and vocabularies. Until recently it was not uncommon to hear that members of the older generation never travelled outside the village of their birth or into which they had married. The festival of L'Mnarja might have been the only exception. Some older people living in inland villages had never travelled from Gozo to Malta or vice versa or even seen the sea!

Another influence (characterised by all our pasta dishes, sweet and savoury pastry dishes, bigilla and other bean dishes) combines both North African and other mediterranean traditions and customs which infiltrated directly or indirectly during the Arab domination of Sicily in 870 AD. Yet there are puzzling questions – why, did only some Arab or North African foods take hold and not others? Why did we continue to import Halwa (known as Ħelwa tat-Tork) but not the savoury tahina which comes from the identical source and forms the basis of a number of exquisite Arab dishes? Tahina has now begun to be imported, but only through the health shop industry which has only a few outlets. Possibly, the strongest influences which differentiate our culinary traditions from those of our closest neighbours, were brought about by the chefs who cooked for the Knights and the French Knights in particular. They will have brought with them the foods and techniques of their own "langues" – in other words, the French provinces and are reflected to this day in our more elaborate meat and fish dishes, our buljut (from the French "bouilli" or pot au feu, għad-dobbu (from en daube), stuffat (from "estouffat") and ħobz biż żejt almost certainly derived from the Provençal Pan Bagn. It is possible that the fondness for adding a proportion of chicory (ċikwejra) to our coffee also stems from this French custom which continues in France to this day. Pamela Parkinson Large has offered us an imaginative description of what the Knights' dining tables might have looked like – the food plentiful and brightly coloured, even sensual perhaps, to compensate for their vows of chastity – "picture the huge tables, shining with silver, groaning and almost bending under the weight of elaborate fantasies; picture fish dancing over beds of gleaming saffron rice." We know that saffron had already been introduced to the islands by the Phoenicians but if the Knights indulged their passion for it, in the quantities claimed, this was, indeed, very conspicuous consumption since the toil involved in the picking and processing of the stamens of the wild crocus (*crocus sativus* – family *Iridaceae*) in order to produce minute quantities of saffron filaments is considerable. The Knights also believed strongly, however, in the properties of food as medicine. As Zeldin (p. 246) (see bibliography) tells us "they all confusedly reconciled war with care for the sick – and gave Malta one of the world's most magnificent hospitals which cared for 700 patients – their sheets changed whenever they needed to be, and their food as outstanding as the personal attention paid to them – rice, vermicelli and herbs, meat, fowl of all kinds, fresh eggs, almonds and sweet biscuits". The very sick were given only the very best and most delicate of foods, whilst those who were stronger had pigeon, game, potatoes and sausages. At one time 200 chickens a day were used just for soup. He adds that the Knights themselves had double portions and, in time, the interests of their institution took precedence over the patients' and the Knights forgot about their compassion.

So what of the Maltese cuisine now? How is it presented to the increasing numbers of non-British tourists? Does it matter? Must we continue, forever, to provide English cafe or pub food so many years after independence? If tourism must be an important element in our economy then the food offered to tourists does matter. It is often argued that tourists are given what they demand. The writer and historian, Ernle Bradford, once complained bitterly to one of us about a sandwich served to him in a Marsalforn bar. "Worse than British Rail" was his comment. The provider was asked why he couldn't have served crusty Maltese bread and he replied, with passion "This is what the tourists want!" Bradford would be pleasantly surprised now – crusty rolls filled with tomatoes and olives are available everywhere and can be delicious. Should not the Maltese tourist board be taking the whole matter much more seriously? Germans don't expect German food when they visit France or England. If good Maltese and other Mediterranean dishes were offered at varying prices would the British tourists go home? We doubt it. As long as food is of high quality, varied and well cooked, we believe that our British visitors would appreciate it much as they do when they visit other countries. At present, many French, German and other tourists must be quite baffled by the average tourist menu. Many of them are aware of our history and are prepared to communicate with us via the English language and to find numerous delightful examples of our recent colonial past such as British telephone boxes and pillar boxes, Queen Victoria's statue and so on; but what must they think of a seaside cafe in central Sliema bearing an Italian name and serving reasonable espressos and Italian cakes while simultaneously advertising "Curried beef, chicken and fish?" Even the British at home are now very knowledgeable about and enjoy genuine Indian food from different parts of the subcontinent. Surely it is not Malta's mission to perpetuate colonial flour-thickened curries, made with stale curry powder, left over meat and a handful of sultanas? Another well known Valletta cafe-overtly Italian in style continues to serve those cotton-wool sandwiches decorated with shredded lettuce and a silly slice of pale tomato as though to compensate for the bread's hideous appearance. A typical dinner menu for package tourists in the 1990s consists of packet asparagus soup, roast lamb, processed peas and a gateau decorated with ersatz cream. This is at a time when fresh peas and exquisite qarabagħli could be bought on every street corner and a number of reputable Maltese confectioners would have been glad to supply genuine almond cakes or kannoli. However, perhaps we miss the point – it is possible that our visitors find these aberrations quaint and charming, in much the same way as block of flats in Sliema are named "The Elms" and "The Oaks" – endearing perhaps, rather than quite ridiculous.

Let us sympathise with the providers – mass tourism exacts certain standards – perhaps many restaurateurs would like to make radical changes to their menus but dare not take the risk. Some critics maintain that many Maltese chefs lack imagination and even that they have little love of cooking. (Interesting to note, therefore, that the great English cookery writer Elizabeth David first grew interested in food "under the influence of a Maltese cook of dazzling ability" (Kininmonth p. 93). Owners are interested only in having a prime position and making huge profits. If chefs were to choose to make changes to their menus and expanding on the Maltese repertoire which is not large, they might consider selecting dishes and techniques from other Southern European, Mediterranean and North African countries to which we are culturally and/or ecologically close. Their traditions and practices would almost certainly have been absorbed by diffusion had Maltese history taken a different turn. Seaside cafes could be offering Maltese variations of couscous or the Turkish Imam Bayildi as a matter of course along with Mqarrun fil-Forn and Braġoli. Cod and chips could vanish forever! That would be a welcome development.

There have been changes for the better. One can now order ħobż-biż-żejt as well as ham and cheese rolls – yet hamburger and hot dog stalls now stand brashly next to the traditional *qubbajt* stalls at our *festi*. Restaurant standards may easily get lowered as staff shortages and semi-absent managers affect the finished product.

Regrettably too, in some restaurants, helpings become smaller as prices rise out of all proportion with other parts of Europe. Local fish of very good quality is often ruined by freezing, poor cooking, re-heating and cheap oil. Ravjul are sometimes so thick you can't chew the edges. We must stress that these criticisms are aimed chiefly at tourist eating places. At the higher price restaurants some very fine cooking is taking place and superb fish dishes can be had.

We don't know what to say about Maltese wine. Would that the contents could approximate to the grandeur of the labels! We do, however, welcome the new range of wines made from imported Italian grapes under a local label, though they are costly when compared with similar products in France or Italy. Perhaps we can admit that our wines today have greatly improved since the days when it used to be said that there was one grape in every bottle.

Malta's health statistics are rather alarming – we are one of the highest smoking nations in the world and it is said that we consume more soft drinks per capita than any other country except America. There is a very high incidence of diabetes and of certain types of cancer and extremely high blood lead levels. The Mediterranean diet should come easily to us and promote longevity and sound health but it has been overlaid by the dietary consequences of Empire. Perhaps we should remind ourselves of the advanced attitude to food and health and the relationship between them upheld by the Knights of Malta in their remarkable hospital.

Cooking in Maltese and Gozitan homes continues to be important to our way of life; recipes are handed down through families and the family meal remains an important occasion for communication and celebration. Now that many married women work outside the home – as well as inside it – some men are beginning to take a more active part in all aspects of home life, sharing in the care of children and everything else, including cooking. Homo Domesticus we salute you! We assure you that you will find cooking for your family a therapeutic activity, especially when we all take turns and no one person has to do it every day. To the growing generation of cooks of both sexes we probably have little to add to what they have learned from their own families, except it is worth remembering that good cooking has a value which transcends the food itself since people come together to communicate and make peace when good meals are shared.

We have waited in many grocery and greengrocery queues and heard comments about the increasingly high cost of living. Yet, for those who would make a determined effort to spend less (or nothing at all) on imported, poor-quality packaged foods (why are grocers' shelves stacked with sliced processed cheese for example?), silly "convenience" foods, squashes and soft drinks and too many cakes, the quite considerable savings thus made should be directed towards good olive oil and moderate quantities of butter, good cheese, fresh coffee and fresh fruit and vegetables in season. Good cooking need not, as is often supposed, require endless hours in the kitchen – the use of food processors combined with thoughtful organisation and advance preparation can be incorporated into a working day and fitted in with other activities.

Visitors who want to learn about our food will find the traditional Maltese loaf unsurpassable – BUT we would like to see the baking industry producing a loaf identical in every way but incorporating a proportion of wholemeal flour – say 30% – for the sake of the nation's health. We have tried this and it works well. Fresh, dry and peppery gbejniet are now more available than they used to be, locally produced pasta is good, but rikotta is on the whole disappointing. Our fruit and vegetables and fruit can be absolutely wonderful and it is noticeable that shoppers (mostly women) expect high standards and select their produce very carefully. Maltese people living abroad often remark that minestras and soups taste much better here despite the fact that identical vegetables are used in England. North America and Australia. Pastizzi remain of exceptionally good quality (despite poor rikotta) delicious and excellent value. The older generation still insists, however, that the quality texture and taste of meat has deteriorated.

In our previous introduction we remarked on the British influence being the most recent but, as we've already remarked, the growing generation is more familiar with the Italian language than the post WW2 generation was. This is largely the influence of Italian television. we speculate that the Italian influence might gain ascendancy over time, whether or not our islands eventually join the European Union. Yet even this is not certain since the impact of countless food programmes on cable television and the world-wide web will also affect our traditions.

Commentators on our first introduction have pointed out to us that the hollowed-out loaf (filled with a ħobż biż-żejt mixture) wrapped in a cloth and sliced with a penknife at the time of eating – so practical and filling for outdoor workers – is now giving way to a more regular sandwich. The tradition has not died out altogether, yet one questions whether one section of society should continue to maintain ancient traditions and look picturesque in order that other sections of society and tourists can admire and photograph them! Other readers have remarked that there is nothing "sweet" about the late 20th century invasion of our islands by estate agents, tourists, tycoons and indigenous developers (demolition fetishists). We were well aware of this at the time of writing and used the word "sweet" quite cynically. Tourism and high-rise blocks are not quite weapons of destruction so, in that sense, the invasion is strictly speaking painless; but we cannot express our horror strongly enough at the attitude of successive governments and their refusal to stop the philistines who would turn Malta into a huge building site. When one considers that old buildings in ancient cities like Assisi have been eradicated by earthquakes and their loss mourned by the inhabitants, should it not make us think again that we are demolishing Malta's history and culture ourselves without the help of a single earth tremor!

Once again we will welcome readers' comments on this new edition and we hope that despite our well-intentioned criticisms, readers will enjoy our recipes and that the young Maltese generation will find our book a useful addition to the knowledge that have already gained from their parents and grandparents.

A Few Facts

◆ Sixty miles south of Sicily in the Mediterranean Sea lie three islands on a NW/SW axis. The largest is Malta, second comes Gozo, and between them sits the smallest: Comino or Kemmuna. The uninhabited rocks of Comminotto and Filfla complete the archipelago. The drift of the land mass is towards the north-east, and Valletta, the chief city, capital and harbour shares that sheltered aspect. Protected, that is, until the 'Gregale' blows from the north-west at the equinox, which has historically caused much damage to ships at anchor, and drowned 600 people in 1555. This wind is the Euroclydon of *The Acts of the Apostles*, the tempest which blew St Paul into Malta on his way under escort to Rome – which happy landing was the occasion of the conversion of the 'barbarous' yet hospitable people to the Christian faith and, later, Roman Catholicism.

A hinge between the eastern and western halves of the Mediterranean, Malta has never been short of occupants. Its prehistory was graced by Late Neolithic henges and rock-cut tombs (the tomb at Hal Saflieni held an estimated 7,000 bodies), and evidence has survived of trade in obsidian with the rest of the Mediterranean basin from the same period. However, that population, which was probably drawn from nearby Sicily, was long ago replaced by the first important colonists, those intrepid Levantine merchants and navigators, the Phoenicians. From the ninth century BC, they cast their net of trading posts along the northern shore of Africa, into Spain and the Balearics, Sardinia and the western end of Sicily, and Malta. Ignore the ambition and drive of Hannibal's Carthage; Phoenicia survived in Malta while it perished elsewhere. Successive conquerors never sought to colonize the islands again, happy to rule and exploit, but never to replace, the population. Hence the Maltese tongue, which has had a shadowy, underground existence through centuries of change and upheaval, has Semitic roots.

When Carthage was defeated by Rome in 218 BC, Malta passed to the republic – as part of the province of Sicily. It remained a prosperous outpost of empire, falling to the Eastern sphere of influence ruled from Byzantium from AD 395, although the church remained attached to the orbit of Rome. So things rested until the Arabs conquered the islands in AD 870: the Greeks cannot have been too popular for the local population joined the invaders in a general massacre of the garrison.

The period of Islamic rule, which lasted until 1090, seems to have been non-intrusive. The Arabs were concentrated around Rabat, but left the inhabitants with their faith and their own customs: a sufficiently lackadaisical occupation for the new Norman kings of Sicily to invade and wrest the land from their control with a very small force indeed, aided and abetted by the local population as had once been the Arabs.

Malta then marched in step with the fortunes of Sicily: the Norman dynasty, a period of French rule under Charles of Anjou, before settling down as part of the Catalan empire of the kings of Aragon after the pusch known as the Sicilian Vespers in 1282. The unlikely heir of these kings in the sixteenth century was the Emperor Charles V, who took the fateful step in 1530 of granting Malta to the crusading order of the Knights of St John, the Hospitallers, who had been ejected from their island fortress of Rhodes by the Ottoman Turks.

The Emperor Charles and much of Europe were preoccupied by the Ottoman threat – think of Don Quixote. To grant Malta to the Knights would have seemed an act both of piety and wise forethought: they may have lost their battle for Rhodes, but they could still act as bastion against further incursions by the infidel. The Order was to prove its valour and fighting spirit in the years immediately after the grant, and its architectural ambitions were happily absorbed by the new foundation of the city and fortress of Valletta, named after Grand Master Jean Parisot de la Valette.

The Knights of Malta were endowed with lands across Europe, and Malta benefited from their occupation in much the same way as in later years the defence and shipping industries were to keep the economy afloat. The indigenous population had grown too large to be self-supporting in food or money, and required an external prop for much of the postmedieval period. As with earlier regimes, the Knights were not much interested in replacing the native population, or even in converting them from their customary way of life; happy in fact to co-exist as a rather effete ruling class that became more and more Francophone and Francophile, and more concerned with the correct quarterings on a knight's escutcheons than anything of more general significance.

It all came to a horrible Republican end in 1798 when Napoleon invaded. The change was revolutionary indeed, to such an extent that the Maltese were horrified to think French influence might persist after the Treaty of Amiens in 1802, and relieved when they passed finally to the British in 1814. The islanders had in fact themselves requested the British to oust Napoleon in 1800. The revolutionary interlude may have been short, but the Code Napoléon survived as a potent legal influence, alongside Canon Law, statute law, government regulations, and common law.

Maltese history has ever been full of tortuous politics marking the uneasy relations between the local inhabitants and their rulers. The British period was no exception, and a close account of the ups and downs between 1814 and the final grant of independence in 1964 would fill many more books than this. The common thread, however, was the essential contribution of the naval dockyards to the economy of the islands, and the importance of Malta's straddling the shipping lanes. This was demonstrated with epic bravery in the trials of the island in the Second World War, under constant attack by Italian and German forces. There were more than 3,000 separate air raids, and the people's valour was recognized by the award of the George Cross in 1942.

In 1947 the British granted self-government, revoked it in 1959, restored it in 1962 and gave full independence two years later.

❖ ❖ ❖ ❖ ❖

Something of the muddle of political history can be seen in the food we describe in this book. The cookery is a mixture of influences, yet with a consistent undertow that has lasted as long as time itself. The same characteristics may be seen in linguistic developments. Although the indigenous population spoke Maltese, it was not an official language, and indeed was not much written, until the last century. It has a Semitic structure. Sporadic attempts were made to adapt the Arabic alphabet to it. Ultimately the unique set of diacriticals for Roman script was devised to reflect the spoken tongue.

The historicist nationalism that was everywhere in Europe during the last century in fact led a strong party in Malta to embrace the Italian language. Latin had been the official language under the Knights of Malta; then, on the simple grounds that Malta was closer to Sicily than Africa, and because it had been a useful place of refuge for Italian dissidents who had a disproportionate political influence on the community, Italian replaced Latin in the courts and was even proposed as the language of education. Fewer than 15 per cent of the population spoke Italian in 1900, yet this was the language they had to master if they fell among lawyers. Maltese-speakers were at a permanent disadvantage.

❖ ❖ ❖ ❖ ❖

The islands have a greater density of population than Jamaica or Martinique in the Caribbean, and this has been a concern for many decades. Even at the turn of the century the total was 206,000, and today it stands at 365,000, although the birth rate is now declining. The majority (85 per cent) lives in towns; only two per cent earn their living from agriculture; one third from manufacturing, mining and construction; and forty per cent from administration, defence and services.

The climate, apart from those winds, is benign: an average temperature of 25°C/77°F in July, 13°C/56°F in January; rainfall, mostly during the winter, is a mere 510 mm. Vegetation on the limestone hills can be sparse, but the islands are full of flowers and flowering shrubs that make the honey as good as any from Mount Hymettus.

Weights and measures

◆ The following are the traditional Maltese weights, with approximate metric and imperial equivalents.

Maltese	*Metric*	*Imperial*
uqija	25–30 g	1 oz
nofs qwart	100 g	3 1/2 oz
kwart	200 g	7 oz
nofs artal	400 g	14 oz
ratal	800 g	1 lb 12 oz
nofs wiżna (2 1/2 ratal)	2 kg	4 lb 6 oz
wiżna (5 ratal)	4 kg	8 lb 12 oz

Another measure, *kejl*, is less frequently encountered these days. It used to be used to measure capers, beans, nuts and similar foods by volume. One *kejla* holds one-tenth of a *siegh*, a measure for grain or land, of Arabic origin. There were three or more standard sizes of the *kejla* and since it was a receptacle it could be used for both solid and liquid measurement.

Ratal derives from a Baghdad weight *rotles*.

The term is used in a recipe Claudia Roden reproduces for *Raghif Alsiniyyeh* – an extraordinary and luxurious pie described by the thirteenth-century scholar Abd-al Latif al-Baghdadi in *Kitab al-ifadah wa'l-l'tibar* as well as appearing throughout the Baghdad cookery book which Professor Arberry translated. He gives *ratl* rather than *rotles* but the comparative weights he gives, from Dr Daoud Chelebi, are not the same as those we know for the Maltese *ratal*. Thus he gives 1 *ratl* = 12 *uqiya* = 1 pint; 1 *uqiya* = 12 *dirham*, and 1 *dirham* = 6 *danaq*.

Other measures still used in Malta are the carat (relating to gold), the term derived from the weight of a seed of the carob pod, and the *dirham*, from the weight of a silver Arabic coin, weighing one-eighth of an ounce.

Weights and measures in the recipes below are metric. As Britain has now moved wholly to the metric system, to continue giving imperial measure is only to slow the learning process. Broadly speaking, 25 g is the equivalent of 1 ounce and 450 g of 1 pound. A pint is 600 ml.

Quantities

The bulk of the recipes are designed for four hungry people. However, many originated from the days when families were large and will often feed six.

Ingredients and technicalities

Lists of ingredients in recipe books often make assumptions that may not be mirrored in the minds of their readers. We take it as axiomatic that readers will use the best quality ingredients, whether we have specified them or not. For instance, chocolate: use the best, with at least 60 per cent cocoa solids; or almond essence: don't have any truck with chemical substitutes. The same for natural products: use organic vegetables where possible, the best quality meat, the freshest fish. These things should not need repeating.

Where we have listed 'pepper' in the recipes, 'freshly ground black pepper' is intended. In the few instances where white pepper is preferable, the fact is recorded.

In like manner, when we specify grated Parmesan, we intend Parmesan cheese bought in the block and freshly grated.

In the many recipes that call for tomatoes, we have specified fresh produce. Often enough, tinned tomatoes are as good, even better than glass-house, winter crops. The reader should feel free to substitute.

Although we may not have stated it at each turn, it is presumed that when we specify an oven at a certain temperature, we mean the oven to be pre-heated.

Where we have hard-boiled eggs incorporated into a pie or other dish, they should be boiled as lightly as possible (just so that they can be peeled) in order that they are not baked to extinction the second time of cooking.

Most of our pies and pastry dishes are not blind-baked. When the filling is inserted in the pastry case, it is wise to ensure it is entirely cold. Warm fillings cause the pastry to become soggy.

In our references to the Maltese vegetable marrow *qarabagħli* we have used the colloquial and modern written plural form which is given by the late Professor Aquilina.

PRONUNCIATION

The Maltese alphabet is composed of 5 vowels and 24 consonants. Diacriticals indicate the pronunciation of certain letters, which may vary depending on their position or their immediate neighbours in a word.

ċ is pronounced 'ch' as in *change*

ġ is pronounced 'dge' as in *judge* or, at the end of a word, as 'tch' as in *fetch*

g is hard, as in go

għ when before or after the vowels *a*, *o* and *e* results in a lengthening of the vowel sound, thus qarabagħli is 'qarabaali'

għ before the vowel *i* changes the sound to 'ay' as in *day*, thus għira is 'ay-ra'

għ before the vowel *u* changes the sound to 'ou' as in *soul* or 'ow' as in *bowl*; thus bgħuda (meaning distance) becomes 'bowda'

h is not pronounced, as in *heir* or *hour*

ħ is pronounced, as in *hot* or *helpful*

q is expressed gutturally, like a strong glottal stop or a 'k' far back in the mouth

x is pronounced 'sh' as in *ship*

z is pronounced 'ts'as in *cats*

ż is pronounced 'z' as in *freeze*

j serves as a consonental 'y' as in *yellow*

SOPOP
SOUPS

If you walk through a Maltese village in the late morning you will notice the irresistible smell of cooking which escapes from almost every house as the big meal of the day is being prepared. It may be *toqlija* – onions, garlic and tomatoes frying in olive oil which is used to form the basis of a tomato sauce to accompany a main dish of spaghetti. Or it may be the all-pervading smell of soup gently simmering. It might be thick, like *minestra*, which is almost a stew, and full of vegetables, pasta and beans, or a rich and nourishing beef broth or a fresh tomato soup. Tinned and packaged products have become a serious challenge to home cooking everywhere, but the preparation of fresh soups still goes on in Malta.

Soups need not take hours and hours to prepare. What is important is that they should simmer for a long time. Maltese kitchens used to boast (and some still do) a small paraffin stove (*kuċiniera*) ideal for slow cooking. Maltese soups are not always a first course, but often a meal in themselves. A soup may be heated up again with an egg poached in it as the only dish for supper (always a light meal if there has been a big lunch). We do not go in so much for strained or creamed soups, and the vegetables are either very finely chopped or coarsely chopped as in *minestra* and *kawlata*, though a notable exception is tomato soup.

Brodu tal-laħam
Beef Broth

1 kg shin of beef and the marrowbone sawn in pieces
1–2 tsp salt
2–3 onions, chopped
2 carrots, chopped
1 stick celery, chopped
1 kohlrabi or turnip, chopped
2 medium potatoes, chopped
1 tsp tomato purée
Pepper
100 g pasta or 50 g rice

◆ Wash the meat, score in 2 or 3 places and place it in a large saucepan with 2 litres of water and salt – this allows the juices to run out and give a rich flavour to the soup. Allow the meat to soak for about an hour. Chop all the vegetables finely. Kohl Rabi belongs to the Brassica family – it is Brassica Oleracea or Caulorapa. The Maltese name for it is ġidra – it has other idomatic interpretations (see Aquilina's dictionary). If using Maltese celery leave it whole, tie it in a bundle and remove at the end of cooking. Maltese celery does not grow thick stalks due to the absence of frost. It is probably the same as the Sicilian 'Sedano' – (apium graveolens of the Apiaceae family). Bring the meat to the boil very slowly and stir in the scum. Add the vegetables, tomato purée and pepper. Cover and allow to simmer very gently for about 3 hours. During the last half hour add the marrow bones and then the rice or pasta for the last 10 minutes. Some cooks prefer to substitute semolina which adds thickening to the soup.

The meat is called *buljut* in Maltese – a word thought to derive from the French 'bouilli' (literally 'boiled'). It is eaten apart from the soup as a separate course. The marrow is extracted from the bone and served on bread, baked bread or toast. The largest portion of this delicacy, or even the whole of it, was traditionally given to the smallest child in the family.

Brodu tal-laħam u tal-ħaxix
Beef and vegetable soup

The ingredients are as in the preceding recipe

◆ The difference between this recipe and the preceding one is that the first gives a really rich broth. The meat soaking in the water ensures the juices leach into the soup – whereas here the meat is placed in boiling water, sealing the juices in. The result is a more succulent *buljut*. If both a rich broth and a good *buljut* are required this can still be achieved by using a smaller piece of shin and following the directions in the previous recipe, then adding a better cut of beef when the soup boils.

Chop all the vegetables finely and place in the boiling water with the meat and salt. The meat should be tied as a rolled joint. Reduce the heat to a simmer. Do not boil. Continue in the same way as in the previous recipe.

Some families like additional potatoes to accompany the *buljut*. In this case, remove the cooked potatoes with a slotted spoon before adding the rice or pasta. *Buljut* is absolutely delicious eaten hot accompanied by boiled potatoes and a *zalza ħadra* (page 218).

Brodu bl-imqarrun
Soup with macaroni

The ingredients are the same as for beef broth above, with the addition of 25–50 g of macaroni per person.

◆ We do not know whether this is a common Maltese recipe but we include it as one which was always popular with the children in our family. Follow either of the preceding recipes, omitting the pasta and rice. During the last 15 or 20 minutes of cooking add about 25–50 g per person of macaroni. When this is cooked serve the soup giving each person a generous portion of macaroni. The family tradition was to eat the soup and vegetables first and then go on to eat the macaroni left in the soup plate with a generous lump of butter and grated Parmesan cheese. This dish makes a complete meal and like so many of our dishes, also economises on fuel.

Tarja bil-butir
Vermicelli soup

75 g tarja *per person*
Salt
Plenty of butter and grated Parmesan or dried ġbejniet
Black pepper
Milk to taste

◆ We are wary about including this recipe, since it is so simple, almost nursery cooking. *Tarja* is the finest pasta, sometimes called angels' hair. Birds' tongues (ilsien l'għasfur) or other fine pasta can be used but *tarja* is traditional.

Cook the *tarja* in boiling salted water until tender (this should take only a very few minutes). Drain and serve in hot bowls with plenty of butter, cheese, salt and pepper.

If you want it to be 'soupy', return the *tarja* to the pan, leaving a little of the cooking liquid, and add a fair quantity of milk. Heat thoroughly. Pour into the bowls and add the remaining ingredients as before. Anglicized toddlers used to like it with a little Marmite.

Brodu tat-tiġieġa
Chicken soup

1 whole trussed chicken which may be stuffed as in the recipe for a stuffing for chicken on page 105–6
The same vegetables as in beef broth, above
50 g rice
1 bay leaf
2 eggs
Salt and pepper
Lemon wedges

◆ Place the chicken in cold water to cover and bring gently to the boil, then add the chopped vegetables and simmer very gently as in *brodu tal-laħam*. If the giblets are to be cooked, add the neck and gizzard at the same time as the chicken but the heart and liver can be added towards the end of the cooking time. Allow approximately 35 minutes to every 400 g of chicken. Add the rice for the last 12 minutes of cooking.

Before serving, beat the eggs well and add a ladle or two of hot soup to them. Distribute this egg and soup mixture amongst your soup bowls and top up with more soup. Do not add the beaten eggs to the simmering soup as this will result in a *straciatella*. Serve with lemon wedges. Normally, the chicken is eaten boiled or briskly fried, whole, in a mixture of butter and olive oil. The reason for the traditional boiling and frying procedure is that most homes used not to have domestic ovens. Communal bread ovens were used for Sunday roasts but not, usually, more frequently than that. We hear that the old Valor ovens are still in use despite the advent of double ovens, and microwaves. Valor ovens rest on top of three paraffin stoves and, as may be imagined, regulating the temperature is a difficult task but can be successful if the cook is patient and prepared to experiment.

Brodu tad-dundjan
Turkey soup

◆ This is made in the same way as chicken soup. The tradition must surely be dying out now, but one can still prepare an excellent turkey soup using the wings, neck and giblets and the usual soup vegetables. In our family it was customary to serve this as a consomme, with sherry and the chopped giblets, instead of timpana, the macaroni pie that was often the heavy prelude to a formal or festive meal.

Soppa tal-għazz
Lentil soup

150 g lentils
1 stick celery (chop the stalk or tie the stalk and leaves into a bunch)
1 onion, chopped
1 kohlrabi, chopped
1 potato, chopped
4 pigs trotters
Salt and pepper
Chopped parsley

◆ Wash the lentils and soak them in water for an hour or so. Bring them to a boil in their soaking water, then drain them and place them with all the other ingredients in a saucepan with a litre of water and bring to the boil. Cook long and gently until the trotters are very tender. Season well. Sprinkle chopped parsley over each serving. The trotters may be eaten hot or cold.

Minestra

Thick vegetable soup

100 g favetta *(fava beans)*
2–3 large onions
3 large potatoes
2 sticks celery
3 carrots
1–2 kohlrabi
Half a cabbage
2–3 qarabagħli *or courgettes*
Half a cauliflower
400 g pumpkin
1 tbsp tomato purée
1 tbsp olive oil
Salt and pepper
100 g thick pasta

◆ Soak the beans for an hour or two and discard the water. Cut up all the vegetables fairly large and place in a large saucepan. Pour on 1500 ml boiling water which should reach about half-way up the pan. Add the tomato purée, oil, salt and pepper. Cover, bring to the boil and simmer very gently for about two hours, stirring occasionally. The *favetta* are perhaps best cooked separately and added to the *minestra* in the last 30 minutes

When all the vegetables are cooked, the *minestra* is best left as it is, but it can be mashed roughly or put through a blender.

Return to the heat, add the pasta and cook for 12 minutes or until tender. In some villages it was customary to add two or three different kinds of pasta (as Italians do in *Tuani e Lampo*, or 'Thunder and Lightning'). A little milk and a knob of butter may be added to each serving at the last moment. Freshly grated Parmesan is offered at the table.

If you have time, you may initially fry the vegetables, add boiling water and proceed as above. *Minestra* varies widely between households and there is much discussion on which vegetables should be included or omitted. Some like to use only one kind of pumpkin, others use both the orange variety which softens and melts, as well as *qara tork* which is pale yellow and retains its firmness. Readers will recognize that *minestra* making is a serious business in Malta and Gozo.

Kawlata

Thick pork and vegetable soup

◆ This thick soup is made in much the same way as minestra but with the addition of a large raw or cooked pork bone or a pig's trotter (*xikel*). Thickly sliced Malta sausages are added about 45 minutes before the end of the cooking. Pasta is not usually added to *kawlata*, neither is it served with grated cheese. Milk and butter are optional. It has been pointed out to us that *kawlata* resembles *la fabada*, a Northern Spanish bean dish, half soup, half stew, to which black pudding is also added at the end of cooking.

Minestra bil-kirxa

Thick vegetable soup with tripe

◆ Prepare a minestra according to the recipe previously given.

Wash and thoroughly clean about 1 kg of tripe by cutting it up with scissors, opening up the tubes and washing in several changes of water acidulated with lemon juice. Add to the *minestra* for the entire cooking time. Some tripe is sold partially cooked, in which case it can be added later in the cooking.

Brodu tal-qafas

Chicken or turkey carcass soup

◆ This does not sound at all appetising, but is delicious, even preferred by some people to soup made with a fresh, uncooked carcass. The chicken should have been roasted or stewed and the carcass may be fried first before being used as the base for the stock. The soup is made in much the same way as chicken soup for which a recipe is given above. The rice, beaten eggs and lemon are used, but tomato purée is usually omitted in the soup made with a cooked carcass. Soups made from bones require long, slow cooking but not too long, otherwise the soup may literally taste of bones.

Soppa tal-qarabagħli
Courgette soup

2 large onions
25 g butter and a little olive oil
2 large potatoes, sliced
1 stick of celery, sliced
1200 g qarabagħli *(or courgettes)*
Salt and pepper
Butter
2 tbsp single cream

◆ Chop the onions roughly and toss them in the butter and oil until they are soft but not golden. Add the sliced potatoes and celery and after about 10 minutes the *qarabagħli* or courgettes, either halved or sliced depending on size. (It is not necessary to use the youngest and most delicate of the crop.) Add water to cover (approximately 1 litre). The soup should be fairly thick. When all the vegetables are tender, blend or process. Check for seasoning. Stir in a generous lump of butter. Although not authentic, cream improves it.

Soppa tal-armla
Widow's soup

(for 4 people
2 onions, sliced
2 potatoes, sliced or chopped
50 g butter
Olive oil
200 g cauliflower florets
1 kg spinach
1 stick celery, chopped
1 kohlrabi, chopped
1 cos lettuce, chopped
1 curly endive, chopped
400 g fresh peas
4 eggs
4 fresh ġbejniet
4 tbsp rikotta
Borage, a small bunch
Salt and pepper

◆ Tradition dictates that all the vegetable used in this soup should be either white or green.

It should be noted that the endive indicated is the curly endive not the Belgian chicory which the French call endive.

Start by tossing the onions in the butter (with a little olive oil). Wash all the vegetables thoroughly, especially the spinach and endive. Add them to the onions, and cook for a few minutes more. Add water to cover and simmer gently for about 2 hours. Just before serving poach the eggs in the soup, and add the *ġbejniet* and *rikotta*. Heat through but do not boil. This process should not take more than a few minutes.

Serve a poached egg, a *ġbejna* and a portion of *rikotta* in each bowl and ladle the soup over this. We are told that the borage is a traditional addition which has been forgotten. It's Latin name is Borago officinalis (Family Boraginaceae) It is also known as 'Starflower' and many medicinal uses have been discovered in recent years.

Aljotta
Fish and garlic soup

3 tbsp olive oil
2 onions, finely chopped
10 cloves of garlic, chopped – you may use more if you wish
600 g tomatoes
1–2 tsp tomato purée
1 bunch fresh chopped marjoram (merdqux)
50 g long grain rice
Salt and pepper
Lemon wedges

◆ This fish soup takes its name from the Italian 'aglio' (garlic), which is its second main ingredient. The dish is a must for garlic-lovers and one of the best soups on the Maltese menu. If the garlic is omitted, or only very little used, then it is no longer an aljotta but still very palatable. It is best, also, not to use any substitute for marjoram*, fresh if possible.

See page 46 for the types of fish suitable for *aljotta*. Small fish can be just covered with water, seasoned with salt and pepper and a squeeze of lemon juice and simmered for about an hour for the flavour to seep into the water. Strain the liquid through a fine sieve pressing the cooked fish with a wooden spoon to extract all the flavour. Discard what is left in the sieve. If making a stock with larger fish than *aljotta* fish, a different approach should be followed. See the recipe for dentex with mayonnaise on page 80. The aim is for about 2 litres of fish stock.

Fry the onion in the olive oil. When it is soft but not brown add the garlic but do not allow it to brown. Add the tomatoes and tomato purée and the chopped marjoram.* Cook gently for about half an hour until it has thickened slightly. Transfer to a large saucepan and add the fish stock and mix well. Boil the rice separately for just 10–12 minutes, strain and add to the soup just before serving. Season with salt and pepper. Serve with lemon wedges.

* marjorana hortensis;
Family: Lamiaceae. The genus is origanum marjorana whereas oregano is of the genus origanum vulgare. Marjoram has a much more delicate flavour.

Soppa tad-tadam
Tomato soup (1)

2 kg tomatoes, chopped
2 sticks celery, chopped
2 large onions, chopped
Bay leaf
Salt, pepper and sugar
Butter
2 tbsp long grain rice

◆ See our note on page 27, above, for our comments on fresh and tinned tomatoes. Put all the ingredients except the rice with 1 litre of water in a pan and boil until the vegetables are tender. Remove the bay leaf. Liquidize or sieve the soup. Reheat, correct the seasoning and add a knob of butter. The rice is cooked separately (10–12 minutes) and added when the soup is reheated. Some cooks add the rice to the soup at the beginning which serves to thicken it. In this case short grain rice would be acceptable. Some omit the rice altogether and serve the soup with croûtons. A custom from the days of Empire was to use sago or tapioca in place of rice.

Soppa tad-tadam
Tomato soup. (2)

2 kg tomatoes, chopped
2 onions, chopped
2 sticks celery, chopped
2 carrots, chopped
4 medium potatoes, chopped
100 g butter
Salt, pepper and sugar
Milk and butter

◆ Chop the vegetables roughly and fry them all (except the potatoes) in the butter. Add the potatoes and 1 litre of boiling water and cook until the potatoes are tender. Liquidize or process the soup, reheat and correct the seasoning. Add a little milk and butter and serve with croûtons.

Smid

Semolina soup

1 tbsp olive oil
3 cloves of garlic, chopped
800 peeled and chopped tomatoes
1 or 2 bay leaves
4 tbsp semolina
Salt and pepper

◆ Fry the garlic lightly in the oil. Add the tomatoes and stir for a few minutes then add 1 litre boiling water and the bay leaves. Simmer for approximately 30 minutes. Sprinkle in the semolina, stir frequently and simmer for a further 15 minutes, taking care to avoid lumps. Season well and serve with a small knob of butter or a little more olive oil.

Semolina is a popular baby food in many parts of the Mediterranean and this very soup is given to growing babies in Malta. The bay leaf is reputed to help bring up wind.

Kusksu

3 tbsp olive oil
2 onions (sliced)
2 cloves garlic
1 tbsp tomato purée
1 kg broad beans in the shell
100 g kusksu pasta, available from all grocers, particularly when broad beans are in season
400 g fresh peas in the shell
2 litres water
Salt and pepper
3 tbsp olive oil

◆ Pronounce the 'u' as in 'book'. The dish may be confused with the North African couscous since the pasta shape does resemble a very coarse couscous. This pasta is available throughout the islands and its small size makes it excellent for soups. In Italian, the pasta is called *acini di pepe* or peppercorns. *Kusksu* is best in May when the broad beans are becoming large and coarse.

Fry the onion and garlic in the hot oil, add the tomato paste and fry a few minutes longer, then add the broad beans. These should be podded, and the individual skins of the beans also removed. Add water to cover and cook gently for about half an hour until the onion is cooked and the beans not quite tender. Add the *kusksu* and continue cooking for a further 10 minutes. Add the peas, stirring frequently as *kusksu* tends to stick to the pan. Cover and turn off the heat and leave for about 10 minutes. To make a complete meal out of this soup add the egg, *ġbejniet* and *rikotta* used in the recipe for Widow's Soup on page 38. A tin of peeled tomatoes may be used instead of the tomato puree and will further improve the flavour. *Kusksu* may be made with frozen beans and peas but we think readers will agree the final result will not be nearly so good since frozen vegetables can impart a very recognizable non-fresh flavour despite advertisers' claims that they are 'freshly picked'.

Soppa tal-qara aħmar

Pumpkin soup

1 large onion, chopped
2 tbsp olive oil
3 tsp tomato purée
700 g pumpkin, peeled and diced
Salt and pepper
75 g semolina
Plenty of freshly grated Parmesan cheese

◆ This soup should be made with coarse semolina but a finer kind will do if this is unobtainable.

Soften the onion in the oil. Add the tomato puree and the pumpkin. Fry gently for 5 minutes, stirring constantly. Add 1 litre of boiling water and the seasoning and cover. Simmer until the pumpkin is cooked. Remove from the heat and break up the vegetables with a potato masher or alternatively blend until smooth. Stir in the semolina carefully so as to avoid lumps. Return to a low heat and simmer very gently for 10 minutes, stirring well. Serve the Parmesan cheese at the table. Croûtons may be added.

Some cooks like to soak the semolina in cold water before adding to the soup, to decrease the risk of its forming lumps. Should they form, however, the processor or liquidizer will remedy the problem.

Ħut
FISH

In most residential areas in Malta the open air market is strategically placed near the parish church and may start as early as 5 a.m. Many older women still do their shopping on the way home from church so the best choice goes to the early risers. Alternatively you may buy fish from vans which visit the streets in the same way as bread and vegetable vans.

Fish sellers (usually women) display the fish in shallow metal pans, and weigh them in old-fashioned hand-held scales. The central market in Valletta (now returned to its original site in Merchants Street but having lost all its charm in the interests of hygiene and modernisation) is undoubtedly the best place for choice. Distances are small so our fish always smells fresh (a change from the off-putting but unavoidable stench in large city markets on the mainland of Europe). Marsaxlokk on a Sunday morning is another excellent place for choice and freshness. It remains one of the least spoilt of our fishing villages, hectic, lively and very colourful.

The best days for buying fish still tend to be Wednesdays and Fridays. Despite the Catholic church's lifting of the ban on meat-eating on Fridays, tradition dies hard and many families continue to uphold the fast. A section of the population (rapidly dying out) is bound by a wartime vow not to eat meat on Wednesdays.

We give below a broad guide to the most suitable ways of cooking our most popular fish and a classification of fish found in Maltese waters.

A word about our most popular fish – the *lampuka* (dolphin fish or dorado); there is even a street in Pawla bearing its name. It is a migrant, the season lasting from August to November. It has a firm white flesh and a golden colour when fresh (hence the name dorado), and also a distinctive flavour which we call 'togħma ta' baħar', 'taste of sea', particularly noticeable when *lampuki* are freshly caught and fried in olive oil.

These are the broad guidelines on the best methods to use. Remember when buying fish to look carefully for the signs of freshness: firm flesh, bright eyes and bright red gills.

Fish suitable for poaching

◆ *Aċċola* (amberjack); *awrata* (gilt-head bream); *ċerna* (grouper); *dentiċi (dentex); dott* (stone bass); *pesce San Pietro* (John Dory); *sargu* (white bream); *spnotta* (bass).

'Poaching' in the oven (correctly speaking not poaching at all, but cooking fish in a foil or greaseproof paper envelope or papillote) gives possibly even better results than poaching in stock or water, as well as being an easier way to deal with large fish. Prepare the fish in the same way as you would for poaching in water. Stuff it with a bread crumb and parsley mixture or place half a lemon and some fresh herbs in the cavity. Measure out a sheet of aluminium foil, greaseproof or baking parchment. Brush liberally with melted butter if the fish is to be eaten hot, or with olive oil if served cold, paying attention to the areas where head and tail are going to lie as they stick easily. Wrap into a loose parcel, securing the joins. Heat the oven to 140°C/275° F/gas 1. Place the parcel on a large baking sheet.

To assess cooking time, remember the theorem advanced by Alan Davidson in his books about fish in the Mediterranean and the Atlantic, 'the time taken [to cook a piece of fish] does not vary in simple proportion to the thickness, but in proportion to the square of the thickness. If it takes 2 minutes to cook a piece of fish 2 cm thick, then a piece 4 cm thick will require 8 minutes not 4 minutes.' In our estimation, 1 hour at a very low temperature should be right for a fish weighing about a kilogram. The cooking time for fish which has been scored is reduced greatly.

When cooked, remove the foil and lay the fish on a dish with all its juices. If it is to be eaten cold, try to have it within a few hours. A fish which has been in the refrigerator all night deteriorates in taste and texture. Poached fish should always be eaten warm – some would argue it is not worth eating cold. Accompany with mayonnaise, made with olive oil and fresh lemon juice.

Fish suitable for baking

◆ *Fanfru* (pilot fish); *kavall* (chub mackerel); *kubrita* or *tunnaċċ* (little tunny); *lampuka* (dolphin fish or dorado); *plamtu* (Atlantic bonito); *mulett* (mullet); *tumbrell* (frigate mackerel).

The usual method for baking is to prepare a layer of peeled potatoes, sliced or halved horizontally, covered with thinly sliced onions and tomatoes. Pour over them 2 or 3 tbsp of olive oil and the same of water. Season with salt and pepper and chopped fresh marjoram or mint. Bake at 90°C/375°/F/gas 5 for about 1 hour. When they are almost done, add the cleaned and prepared fish. You may stuff the cavity with soft white bread crumbs, parsley, garlic and grated lemon rind, and perhaps some chopped olives or capers, but don't add too many flavours. Pour over a little more oil, season, and bake until both fish and potatoes are cooked. When cooked, the eyes of the fish look white and hard.

Fish suitable for frying

◆ Fanfru (pilot fish); *imsell* (garfish); *kaħlija* (saddled bream); *kavall* (chub mackerel); *lampuka* (dolphin fish); *pixxispad* (swordfish); plamtu (Atlantic bonito); *rużetta* (cleaver wrasse); *sawrell* (scad); *trill* (red mullet); *vopa* (bogue).

Fry small fish whole and cut large ones into steaks. In both cases a coating of flour is all that is needed. Fry in very hot oil, drain on absorbent paper and serve with slices of lemon.

Fish suitable for *aljotta*

◆ *Burqax* (painted comber); *gallina* (grey gurnard); *għarusa* (rainbow wrasse); *ħamiema* (white skate); *skorfna* (small-scaled scorpion fish); *sparlu* (annular bream); *tirda* (green wrasse); *traċna* (spotted weaver).

All the fish listed as suitable for poaching may also be used for *aljotta*, provided one attaches great care not to overcook them. Keep the soup simmering, not boiling. Lift them out carefully. Smaller fish need to be handled carefully too, as some, like *traċna*, have hidden bones which can puncture your fingers.

Fish suitable for stewing

◆ *Gringu* (conger eel); *lampuka* (dolphin fish); *mazzola* (common spiny dogfish); *morina* (moray eel).

Slice 2 or 3 onions and cook gently in olive

oil, add a little wine or water, then the fish, sliced into rounds. Season, cover, and cook slowly for about 20 minutes.

A classification of fish in Maltese waters

Our original reason for producing this table of fish names was that we felt readers would be glad to have it to hand when buying or eating fish as assistance in establishing the Maltese names. However, once we started our research, it soon became clear that the Mediterranean fish waters were (metaphorically) muddy indeed. Some of our readers, along with scholars of the subject, will at times disagree with us, but we proceeded in the belief that many readers will find the table helpful and interesting, even where incomplete. We take responsibility for omissions and inaccuracies.

The study of Mediterranean fish was, until very recently, fraught with confusion, chiefly because of the enormous number of varieties and sizes to be found, and the different views amongst scholars about how to categorize them. A complex argument goes on, for example, about what is and what is not a sardine.

What is more, while the anchovy belongs to the same order (*Clupeiformes*) as the sardine, some would place it in a different family. Fishermen don't help our understanding very much. They know their fish inside out, and confuse things further, for us, by adopting nomenclatures of their own. This is because of minute differences between one fish and another which are no longer recognisable (to the non-fisherman) when we come to buy, let alone cook them. In Malta, we sometimes use familiar Italian names for a fish when a Maltese name already exists, and thus confuse ourselves by thinking we are talking about two different fish. Often, different names are given to fish purely on the basis of size. So, while in theory, the scientific work of cataloguing and naming is complete, the wealth and immense variety of fish, and their names, continue to fascinate as well as confuse the lay person.

We have used a number of sources to help us compile our table and found some puzzling disagreements amongst them. Some scholars describe, name and categorize only edible fish; others have listed every size and species, edible or not. To those who wish to follow the subject further, we recommend the United Nations Food and Agriculture Organization's catalogue and, for an outstanding and excellent illustrated work of classification, combined with marvellous recipes, *Mediterranean Seafood* by Alan Davidson.

In the table which follows we give first the Maltese name, followed by the Latin scientific name, in italics, for the genus, followed by the species. The second Latin name, not in italics, is the relevant family. When more than one Latin name is given, it is because different naturalists have given different names. This is, probably, where some of the confusion begins since both names can be used for the same fish. Thereafter, we give the Italian, French and English names (in that order), and follow those with any other names which we think are relevant, particularly Tunisian Arabic, where it resembles the Maltese.

Since this is a cookery book (and nothing more) the emphasis is on fish to eat, though some inedible ones may have swum in. It is not fully comprehensive of every fish in the Maltese waters. For that, see the excellent work by Guido G. Lanfranco.

AĊĊOLA; *Seriola dumerili, Carangidae; ricciola* (It.); *seriole* (Fr.); amberjack. Best for grilling, baking and stock. A young *aċċola* is called a *ċervjola*.

AJKLA; *Myliobatis aquila*, Myliobatidae; *aguila di mare* (It.); eagle ray; possibly uncatalogued.

ALONGA; *Thunnus alalunga*; Tunnidae; *alalonga* (It.); *germon* (Fr.); little tunny or albacore. A versatile firm-fleshed fish which can be cooked in many ways; the stomach is considered the best part.

ARTIKLA; *Anemonia sulcata; ortie de mer* (Fr.); sea anemone. It is a beautiful, flower-like sea creature. This and others like it belong in a category of their own. Prize them out of their dens with a knife or your thumbs, rinse well to remove all grit, then fry in beaten egg or batter.

ARZNELLA; (or MUNQARA, female); *Maena smaris*, Centracanthidae; *zerro* (It.); *picarel* (Fr.); picarel. Opinions on this fish vary. It is highly valued in some parts of the Mediterranean.

AWRATA; *Sparus aurata* or *Chrysophrys aurata*, sparidae; *orata* (It.); *daurade*, or *dorade* (Fr.); gilt-head bream; ourata (Tunisian). A very highly prized fish; it may be cooked whole and may be stuffed. Bake it whole, poach, or grill in fillets.

BAKKALJAW; This is the Maltese name for salt cod. Cod itself is not found in the Mediterranean. Compare the Spanish *bacalao*, and the Italian *baccalá*. Numerous recipes exist.

BALLOTRA; *Gaidropsarus mediterraneus*, Gadidae; *motella* (It.); *mostelle* (Fr); three-bearded rockling; uncatalogued. A good, dark-fleshed fish. Must be cooked very soon after it is caught.

BAQRA; *Mobula mobular*, Monulidae; *diavola di mare* (It.); devil fish. Nothing could be traced about this fish (which is very rare), so it probably has no culinary value whatever.

BARBUN; *Platichthys flesus flesus*, Pleuronectidae, *passera pianuzza* (It.); *flet* (Fr.); flounder or fluke.

BARBUN IMPERJALI; *Psetta maxima* or *Rhombus maximus*, Bothidae; *rombo chiodato* (It.); *turbot* (Fr.); turbot. An excellent fish, which may be poached or grilled.

BARBUN TAL-GĦAJN; *Bothus podas*, Bothidae; *romp di rena* (It.); no French or English term, except possibly wide-eyed flounder. Frying is probably best.

BARBUN TAT-TBAJJA; *Pleuronectes platessa*, Pleuronectidae; *passera* (It.); plaice. Not really a Mediterranean fish.

BAŻUGA; *Pagellus acarne*, Sparidae; *pagello bastardo* (It.); *pageot blanc* (Fr.); bronze or Spanish bream. For cooking see *pagella* below. Marinading improves this drier version of *pagella*. Use olive oil and lemon juice.

BAŻUGA KAĦLIJA; *Pagellus bogaraveo*, Sparidae; *rovello* (It.); *bogaravelle* (Fr.); blue-spotted bream. Grill the larger ones, otherwise use for soup.

BIES; *Dactylopterus volitans*, Dactylopteridae; *pesce civetta* (It.); *hirondelle* (Fr.); flying gurnard.

BOLL and BOLL TORK; *Dasyatis pastanica* or *violacea*, Dasyatidae; *pastinaca* or *trigone viola* (It.); common sting-ray or blue sting-ray.

BUDAKKRA TAL-QAWWI; *Blennius gattorugine*, Blennidae; *bavosa* (It.); *baveuse* (Fr.); blenny.

BUDAKKRA BŻARIJA; *Tripterygion tripteronotus*, Tripteridigae; *bavosa* (It.); *baveuse* (Fr.); blenny. Best used in soups. This species includes a range of small fish, the largest of which is about 20 cms long.

BURQAX; *Serranus scriba*, Serranidae; *sciarrano, scrittura* (It.); *serran écriture* (Fr.); painted comber. May be used in soups or fried. Note the references to writing in all the names, this refers to its marks which look like scribbles.

BUSUF; *Monoghirus hispidus*, Solidae; *sogliola pelosa* (It.); *sole velue* (Fr.); whiskered sole. Uncatalogued, too small to be of any interest.

BUWAĦĦAL; *Lepadogaster*, Gobiidae; *succhiascoglioe* (It.); cling-fish.

BUXIĦ; (see also *marzpan*); *Crenilabrus mediterraneus*, Labridae. Not of culinary interest, but can always be used in soup.

CAMPERLUNA; *Galeus melastomus*, Scyliorhinidae (see *gattarell*, below). Other names are *bocca-negra* (It.); *chien espagnol* (Fr.); blackmouthed dogfish. Considered even less good than *gattarell*.

ĊAWLA; *Chromis chromis, probably Pomacentridae; castagnola* (It.); *castagnole* (Fr.); blue-damsel fish.

ĊERNA; *Epinephelus guaza*, Serranidae; *cernia*; (It); *mérou* (Fr); grouper; *mennani ahmar* (Tunisian). A superb fish which may be cooked in numerous ways. The central section is good for steaks. Of gentle flavour and firm of flesh, there are many fine recipes for it from all over the Mediterranean.

ĊERVJOLA: see *aċċola*.

ĊIPPULLAZZA; *Scorpaena scrofa*, Scorpaenidae; *scorfano rosso* (It.); *rascasse rouge* (Fr.); largescaled scorpion fish; *bou keshesh ahmar* (Tunisian). If you ever want to try making *bouillabaisse* this is one of the best fish to include; otherwise, bake it.

DENTIĊCI; *Dentex dentex*, Sparidae; *dentice* (It.); *dente* (Fr.); dentex; *dendiq* or *qattous* (Tunisian). With *lampuka*, the most loved Maltese fish. It is wonderful baked or poached. Try grilling or stuffing it for a change.

DOTT; *Epinephelus alexandrinus* or *Polyprion americanum/cernum*, Serranidae; *cernia dorata* or *cernia abadeco/di fondale* (It.); *badèche* or *cernier* (Fr.); wreckfish or stone bass. A versatile and delicious fish which can be prepared in any number of ways. See also *ħanzir*.

DRAGUNETT; see *wiżgħa tal-bahar*.

FANFRU; *Naucrates ductor*, Carangidae; *pesce pilota* (It.); *poisson pilote* (Fr.); pilot fish. This fish is fairly common around Malta but less in other parts of the Mediterranean The Turkish name for it is *malta palamadu*. Suitable for grilling. Traditionally. it is cooked in sea water.

FARFETT; *Gymnura altavela*, Dasyatidae: *altavela* (It.); butterfly ray.

FENEK; *Chimaera monstroso*, Chimaeridae; *chimera* (It.); rabbit fish.

FJAMMA; *Trachypterus trachyprerus*, Trachypteridae; *pesce nastro* (It.); deal fish.

FJAMMA ĦAMRA; *Cepola rubescens*, Cepolidae; cepola (It.); *cépole rougeâtre (Fr.); red-band fish. Best used for soups.*

FJAMMETTA; *Gymnammodytes cicerellus*, Ammodytidae; *cicerello* (It.); *cicerelle* (Fr.); sand-eel or sand-lance. Nothing special, best fried.

GABDOLL; *Cetorhinus maximus*, Squalidae; *squalo elefante* (It.); basking shark.

GALLINA GRIŻZA; *Eutriglia gurnardus*, Scorpaenidae; *cappone gurno* (It.); *grondin gris* (Fr.); grey gurnard Tunisian as below. For cooking, see below.

GALLINELLA or GALLINA; *Triglia lucerna*, Scorpaenidae; *cappone gallinella* (It.); *grondin galinette* (Fr.); tub-gurnard; *serdouq* (Tunisian). For cooking see *gallinetta*, which is smaller.

GALLINETTA; *Triglia lyra*, Scorpaenidae; *cappone lira* (It.); *grondin lyre* (Fr.); piper. May be cooked in a number of ways but perhaps best poached or baked covered with wine in order to introduce some moisture.

GALLINETTA TAR-RIGI; *Trigloporus lastoviza*, Scorpaenidae; *cappone dalmato* (It.); *grondin imbriago* (Fr.); rock or streaked gurnard. Cooking as above.

GANDOFFLI or TAMAR TAL-BAĦAR; *Venus verrucosa*; *tartufo di mare* (It.); *praire* (Fr.); warty Venus. May be eaten raw (but see note on *rizzi* and *artikli*).

GATTARELL and GATTARELL TAR-RUKKAL; *Scyliorhinus caniculus* and *stellaris*, Squalidae. The distinction is between sizes, thus *gattucciol gattopardo* (It.); *petitelgrande roussette* (Fr.); rough hound or nurse hound; *kalb bahrl qattous* (Tunisian). The smaller variety tastes better but needs imaginative cooking.

GĦARUSA; *Coris julis*, Labridae; *donzella* (It.); crénilabre (Fr.); wrasse or corkwing. Fry the largest ones, otherwise use for soup. Għarusa is Maltese for bride. See also *tirda pagun*, below, which are even smaller.

GĦASFUR; *Myliobatis bovinus*, Rajidaei *vaccarclla* (It.); bull ray.

GREMXULA (TAL-BAĦAR ĦOXNA); *Syngnathus acus*, Syngnathidae; *pesce ago* (It.); great pipefish. Probably not edible.

GRINGU TAL QAWWI; *Conger conger*, Congridae; *grongo* (It.); *congre*; (Fr.) conger eel. Highly esteemed in some parts of the Mediterranean and often used in *bouillabaisse*. Try braising with butter, onions and white wine.

GRINGU TAR-RAMEL; *Echelus myrus*, Ophichtidae; *miro* (It.); worm eel.

GURBELL; *Umbrina cirrosa* or *Sciaena cirrose*, Sciaenidae; *ombrina* (It.); *ombrine* (Fr.); ombrine. Bake, fry or grill; North Africans use it in couscous.

GURBELL RAR; *Argyrosomus regium* or *Sciaena aquila*, Sciaenidae; *bocca d'oro* (It.); *maigre* (Fr.); meagre. Firm white flesh which may be baked or poached.

GURBELL TORK; *Corvina nigra* or *Sciaena umbra*, Sciaenidae; *corvo* (It.); *corb* (Fr.); no English term but similar to meagre (above). May be fried or braised with white wine.

ĠURDIEN TAL-FOND; *Coelorhynchus coelorhynchus*, Macrouridae; *pesce sorcio* (It.); soldier fish.

GURDIEN TAL-WARDA; *Hoplostethus mediterraneus*, Zeidae; *pesce specchie* (It.); *poisson montre* (Fr.). They may be noticed by their red colour and are used in soups;

ĦAMIEMA; *Raja alba*, Rajidae; *razza bianca* (It.); raie blanche (Fr.); white skate.

ĦANŻIR (see also *dott*); *Polyprion americanum*, Serranidae; *cernia di fondale* (It.); *cernier* (Fr.); wreckfish or stone bass. Suitable for all methods of cooking, free of bone, delicious and firm fleshed. *Ħanzir* means pig in Maltese.

ĦMAR; *Balistes carolinensis* (or *capriscus*), Balistidae; *pesce balestra* (It.); *baliste* or *cochon de mer* (Fr.); trigger fish; *pisci porcu* (Sicilian); *hallouf bahr*, 'pig of the sea' (Tunisian). Opinions vary on the qualities of this fish. Remove tough skin before cooking. Perhaps best stewed. *Ħmar* means donkey in Maltese.

ĦUTA KAĦLA; *Prionace glauca*, Serranidae; *verdesca* (It.); *peau bleu* (Fr.); blue shark. Davidson tells us that this is sometimes passed off as tunny.

IMSELLA; *Belone bellone*, Belonidae; *aguglia* (It.); *aiguille* or *orphie* (Fr.); garnish; m'sella (Tunisian). Can be fried or braised in a tomato sauce. The backbone becomes a startling green when cooked.

INĊOVA; *Engraulis encrasicolus*, Clupidae; *acciuga* or *alice* (It.); *anchois* (Fr.); anchovy. Delicious fried when very fresh.

INGWATA LIXXA; *Arnoglossus laterna* or *Pleuronectes laterna*, Bothidae; *suacia* (It.); *fausse limande* (Fr.); scaldfish. Best fried.

INGWATA TAL-FAXX; *Arnoglossus grohmann* or kessleri, Bothidae; *suacia fosca* (It.); Grohmann's scaldfish.

INGWATA TAL-GĦAJN; *Solea occellata*, Soleidae; *sogliola occhiuta* (It.); *sole ocellée* (Fr.); eyed sole. May be adapted to every kind of cooking and is extremely delicate. *Għajn* is eye in Maltese.

INGWATA TAL-ISKWAMI; *Citharus linguatula*, Bothidae; *linguattola* (It.); *fausse limande* (Fr.); English name uncertain, possibly spotted flounder. Best fried. *Skwami* is the Maltese word for scales.

KAĦLIJA; Oblada melanura, Sparidae; *occhiata* (It.); *oblade* (Fr.); saddled bream; *kahlaia* (Tunisian). May be grilled, fried or poached.

KASTARDELLA; *Scomberesox saurus*, Belonidae; *costardello* (It.); *balaou* (Fr.); saury or skipper.

KAVALL; *Scomber japonicus colias*, Scombridae or Scomberomoridae; *lanzado* or *sgombro cavallo* (It.); *maquereau espagnol* (Fr.); chub mackerel. A very nourishing fish and good to taste, though not everyone likes the oiliness. Grill, poach or braise in white wine.

KELB ABJAD; *Carcharodon carcharias*, Squaliformes. It may be known by the same French, Italian and Tunisian names as the following entry. In English it is the white shark. This is the really dangerous shark.

KELB IL-BAĦAR; *Galeorhinus galeus*, Squaliformes; *canesca* (It.); *milandre* (Fr.); tope. Not considered the most edible of this family. The French *chien de mer*, Italian *pesce cane* and Tunisian *kalb* (or *kelb*) *bahr* are all in this species and there is some muddle about the names.

KUBRITA (or TUNNAĊĊ); *Euthynnus alletteratus* or *Thynnus thunnina*, Thunnidae; *tonnetto* or *alletterato* (It.); *thonine* (Fr.); little tunny. Different names might indicate younger specimens. For cooking see *alonga*.

KURAZZA; *Sphyrna zygaena*, Squalides; *pesce martello* (It.); *requin marteau* (Fr.); common hammerhead; *ghajn fi garnou* (Tunisian).

KURUNELLA; (1) *Argentina sphyraena*, Argentinidae; *argentina* (It.); *argentine* (Fr.); argentine. Best fried. (2) *Atherina mochon*, *hepsetus* or *boyeri*, depending on cataloguer, Atherinidae; *latterino* (It.); *prêtre* (Fr.); Caspian sand smelt. Fry in olive oil with parsley and garlic.

LAĊĊA; *Alosa-alosa*, Clupidae; *alosa* (It.); allice shad. Best baked, grilled or fried, with or without batter.

LAĊĊA TAL-FAXX; *Sardinella aurita*, Clupidae; *alaccia* (It.); *allache* (Fr.); gilt sardine.

LAĊĊA TAT-TBAJJA; *Alosa falax nilotica* or *Clupea finta*, Clupidae; *cheppia* (It.); *alose feinte* (Fr.); shad or twaite shad. *Tbajja* refers to its spots or, literally, stains. A bony kind of fish best grilled or fried.

LAMPUKA; *Coryphaena hippurus*, Coryphaenidae; *lampuga* (It.); *coriphène (Fr.); Dorado* (Sp); dolphin fish. In some ways the most loved of Maltese fish, though not the grandest.

LAMPUKA TORKA; *Centrolopus niger*, Centrolophidae; *ricciola di fondale* (It.); black-fish.

LIPP; *Molva molva* or *Molva macropthalma*, Belonidae or Exocoetidae; *molva occhiana* (It.); *lingue* (Fr.); blue, Spanish or Mediterranean ring. Stew or fry in chunks.

LIPP TAL-QAWWI, LIPP ABJAD; *Phycis phycis* or *blennioides* (similar), Belonidae or Exocoetidae; *mustella* (It.); *mostelle de fond* (Fr.); fork-beard. These small fish are best fried.

LIZZ; *Sphyraena sphyraena*, Sphyraenidae; *luccio marino* (It.); brochet de mer (Fr.); barracuda. Fry in fillets, or poach whole.

LIZZ TAT-LVANT; *Sphyraena chrysotaenia*, Sphyraenidae. Similar to above with larger eyes. Lanfranco tells us it appears to be entering the Mediterranean from the Suez Canal.

MAKKU; *Aphia minuta*, Gobiidae, also listed under *Brachyocirus pellucidus*; *rossetto nonnati* (It.); *nounat* (Fr.); transparent goby or pellucid sole. *Makku* used to be more easily obtainable. Delicious crisply fried. The whole fish is eaten in the same way as the English whitebait which belongs to the *Sprattus sprattus*, Clupeidae family, see *sardina hadra*, below.

MANKANA; *Gadus trisopterus capelanus* or *Gadus minutus*, Gadidae; *merluzzo cappellano* (It.); *capelan* (Fr.); poor cod. Tends to have a lot of bones but the flavour is good.

MARZPAN; *Sparisoma cretense*, Scaridae; *scaro* (It.); parrot fish. Not catalogued as edible.

MAZZOLA; *Squalus acanthias*, Squalidae; *spinarolo* (It.); *aiguillat tacheté (Fr.); spur dog.*

MAZZOLA BLA-XEWKA; *Mustelus mustelus*, Triakidae; *palombo* (It.); émissole (Fr.); smooth hound. Can be cooked in a variety of ways, or used for soup. Some say it resembles veal. *Bla-xewka* means without prickles or bones.

MAZOLLA TAL-FANAL; *Etmopterus spinax*, Squalidae; *sagri nero* (It.); lantern shark.

MAZZOLA TAT-TBAJJA; *Mustelus asterias*, Squalidae; *palombo stellato* (It.); *émissole* (Fr.); stellate smooth hound. May be stewed and served in a sauce, or fried. This species is differentiated from *Mustelus mustelus* by the many spots (or stains, in Maltese).

MAZZUN; *Gobius paganellus*, Gobiidae; *ghiazzo paganello* (It.); *gobie* (Fr.); rock goby. There are many species. Fry them.

MAZZUN ISWED; *Gobius niger*, Gobiidae; *ghiozzo nero* (It.); *gobie noir* (Fr.); goby. Best fried. Opinions vary about this species, there are numerous varieties, much loved in some Mediterranean countries.

MINFAĦ; *Capros aper*, Caproidae; *pesce tamburo* (It.); boar-fish.

MGĦOŻA; *Puntazzo puntazzo*, Sparidae; *sarago pizzuto* (It.); *sar tambour* (Fr.); sheepshead bream. A fairly ordinary and quite bony fish. *Mgħoża* is the Maltese for goat.

MOLA OR QAMAR; *Mola mola*, Molidae; *pesce luna* (It.); ocean sunfish. *Qamar* is the Maltese for moon

MORINA; *Murena helena*, Muraenidae; *murena* (It.); *murène* (Fr.); moray eel. Opinions vary on its culinary value. Some think it only suitable for *bouillabaisse* while others regard it as one of the finest Mediterranean fish. Try it grilled or poached but omit the bony tail.

MULETT TAL-ISWED; *Mugil cephalus*, Mugilidae; *cefalo* (It.); *mulet cabot* (Fr.); common grey mullet. A very good fish. Grill the small ones and bake the large ones, stuffed if you like. Davidson tells us they go well with couscous. The roe is a delicacy in many parts of the Mediterranean.

MUNGUS; *Lithognatus mormyrus*, Sparidae; *marmora* (It.); *marbré (Fr.); striped bream. Excellent grilled.*

MUNQARA: see *arznega*.

MURRUNA SEWDA; *Hexanchus griseus*, Hexanchidae; six-gilled shark. There is also a seven-gilled shark.

MURRUNA SEWDA; *Dalatias lichia*, Squalidae; *negra* (It.); darkie charlie; Could be related to Lichia amia.

MURRUNA TAX-XEWK; *Echinorhinus brucus*, Squalidae; *ronco* (It.); spiny shark.

NEMUSA; *Sardina pilchardus*, Clupidae; *sardina* (It.); *sardine* (Fr.); pilchard (the English name of the adult fish). *Nemusa* describes the young of this fish, again similar to *makku* but belonging in a different family. In Gozo, *nemusa* are sometimes used as a pizza topping, but possibly *makku* are too. The word *nemusa* also means mosquito in Maltese.

PAĠELLA ĦAMRA; *Pagellus erythrinus*, Sparidae; *fragolino* (It.); *pageot rouge* (Fr.); pandora. Red in colour. Good to fry, grill or bake.

PAĠELLA TAL-GARĠI; *Pagellus centrodontus*, Sparidae; *occhialone* (It.); *dorade commune* (Fr.); red bream. Cooking as above.

PAGRU; *Pagrus pagrus*, Sparidae; *pagro* (It.); *pagre commun* (Fr.); Couch's sea bream. Very good whether baked whole or cut in steaks for baking or grilling.

PANJOL; *Chloropthalmus agassizi*, Synodidae, Order Myctophiformes; *occhione* (It.); greeneye. It has large green eyes at the top of its head. Probably best fried.

PARPANJOL; *Labrus bimaculatus*, Labridae; *tordo fischietto* (It.); *vieille coquette* (Fr.); cuckoo wrasse. All right for soup.

PARTUN; *Scopthalmus rhombus* or *Rhombus laevis*, Bothidae; *rombo liscio* (It.); *barbue* (Fr.); brill. An exceptional fish which adapts to many different ways of cooking. Worth taking trouble over and serving with a delicate sauce, such as hollandaise.

PASTARDELLA; *Tetrapturus belone*, Istiophoridae; *aguglia imperiale* (It.); spearfish (uncommon in the Mediterranean).

PELAMIT; *Euthynnus pelamis*, Thunnidae; *tonnetto listato* (It.); *bonite à ventre rayé (Fr.); skipjack or oceanic bonito. This is the tunny fish one meets in tins. Fresh, it is a firm, meaty and fairly heavy fish, appropriate for baking, grilling and so forth.*

PETRICA and PETRICA TAT-TBAJJA; *Lophius budegassa* or *piscatorius*, depending on size, Lophiidae; *rana pescatrice* or *rospo* (It.); *baudroie* or *lotte* (Fr.); angler fish or monkfish. Cooking the tail is best.

PIXXI KERNUT or KORNUTA; *Peristedion cataphractum*, Peristediidae; *pesce forca* (It.); *malarmat* (Fr.); armed gurnard; *serdouk* (Tunisian) means, literally, cockerel. Try cutting into sections, poaching and serving with any kind of tomato or other braising sauce. The word *kernut* (related to horns) means cuckold in Maltese, while *kornuta* refers to the cuckolded wife.

PIXXILUNA; *Brama brama* or *Brama rayi*, Bramidae; *pesce castagna* (It.); *brème de mer* (Fr.); Ray's bream; Sicilian, *pisci luna*. Certainly a worthwhile fish; may be cooked in a variety of ways.

PIXXI PLAMTU; *Lamna nasus* or *cornubica*, Lamnidae; *smeriglio* (It.); *taupe* (Fr.); porbeagle shark. Good steaks not dissimilar to *pixxispad*.

PIXXI PORKU; *Oxynotus centrina*, Oxynotidae; *pesce porco* (It.); angular rough shark. *Porku* is Maltese for pork.

PIXXI SAN PIETRO; *Zeus faber*, Zeidae; *pesce San Pietro* (It.); *Saint-Pierre* (Fr.); John Dory. An outstanding, delicious fish. Its name has various explanations related to St Peter. Its appearance is forbidding, but the flesh is superb to eat and may be filleted and cooked in a number of ways.

PIXXISPAD; *Xiphias gladius*, Xiphiidae; *pesce spada* (It.); *espadon* (Fr.); swordfish. One of the most loved and commonly found fish in Malta. Frozen, it loses all flavour and texture. Usually eaten as grilled steaks, simply dressed with lemon juice and fresh herbs.

PIXXITONDU; *Isurus oxyrinchus*, Lamnidae; *ossirina* (It.); mackerel shark.

PIXXITRUMBETTA; *Macroamphosus scolopax*, Macroramphosidae; pesce trombetta (It.); snipefish.

PIXXIVOLPI; *Alopias vulpinus*, Alopiidae; *pesce volpe* (It.); thresher shark.

PIZZUNTUN; *Scomber scomnbrus*, Scombridae; *sgomoro* (It.); *maquereau* (Fr.); Atlantic mackerel. Like most fish in this family, it is very oily. Grill or bake.

PLAMTU; *Sarda-sarda* or *Pelamys sarda*, Scomberomoridae; *palamita* (It.); bonite à dos rayé (Fr.); Atlantic bonito; *balamit* (Tunisian). Grilled, fried or baked (whole or in steaks).

QAWSALLA; *Siganus rivulatus*, Siganidae; rabbit fish or spine-foot. Lanfranco tells us this fish is spreading from the Red Sea and Davidson points out that many were found in the Suez Canal when it was closed after 1956.

RAJA TAL-FOSOS; *Raja clavata*, Rajidae; *razza chiodata* (It.); *raie bouclée* (Fr.); thornback ray. Probably the best of the rays. Only the wings are eaten. In France it is prepared with black butter. One of few fish which need not be eaten completely fresh.

RAJA TAR-RAMEL; *Raja radulla or quadrimaculata*, (See also *Raja melitensis* or miraletus), Rajidae; *razza quattrocchi* (It.); *raie miroir* (Fr.); rough ray; *hassira* or *sajjeda* or *hammiema* (Tunisian). Not as good as the preceeding entry. It may be confused with *raja lixxa* (English, brown ray). Lanfranco also lists *raja tal-kwiekeb* and *petruza*, but not all the rays and skates are worth eating. The term 'skate' in English is usually reserved for the larger species. In America 'ray' is only used for the electric varieties, e.g. the stingback. Another example is our *ħaddiela tal-għajnejn* (species *Torpedo torpedo*).

RAŻUN or RUŻUN, also known as LUDHI; *Thalassoma pavo*, Labridae; *donzella pavonina* (It.); ornate wrasse.

REBEKKIN; *Raja oxyrhyncus*, Rajidae; *razza monaco* (It.); long-nosed skate. See the note on rays. On land in Malta, *rebekkin* is the word for the carpenter's brace, used for drilling holes.

REBEKKIN SKUR; *Raja batis*, Rajidae; *razza bavoza* (It.); flapper skate. See above.

REMORA; *Remora remora*, Echeneididae; *remora* (It.); shark sucker. Regarded as not suitable for eating by Aristotle or Pliny (we are told by Alan Davidson) though Pliny considered it suitable for pregnant women. Try stewing.

RIZZA; *Paracentrotus lividus*; *riccio di mare* (It.); *oursin* (Fr.); sea urchin. *Rizzi* abound in rocky seabeds and underwater fishermen bring them up in large quantities. The male *rizzi*, known as *patrijiet* (monks) are not eaten. The females are eaten alive, you prize them open horizontally and eat the bright orange centre with perhaps a squeeze of lemon. Two warnings: we do not believe Maltese *rizzi* are safe to eat in these polluted days; be careful not to step on a *rizza*, not only are the spikes extremely painful but they can start an infection requiring antibiotic treatment.

RONDINELL; *Cypselurus rondeleti* or *Exacoetus rondeleti*, Exocoetidae; *pesce volante* (It.); *poisson volant* or *hirondelle de mer* (Fr.); flying fish. Not at all wonderful to eat.

RUVETT; *Ruvettus pretiosus*, Gempylidae; *ruvetta* (It.); scourer.

RUŻETTA; *Xyrichthys novacule*, Labridae; *pesce pettine* (It.); cleaver wrasse. See also *rażun* (ornate wrasse).

SALLURA; *Anguilla-anguilla*, Synonidae; *anguilla* (It.); *anguille* (Fr.); common eel.

SARDINA ĦADRA; *Clupea sprattus* or *Sprattus sprattus*, Clupidae; *papalina* (It.); sprat (Fr.); sprat. Though the sprat is larger than the anchovy, it is inferior. The English whitebait are very small sprats; *brislıng* in Norwegian. Not to be confused with *makku* (see above) although they may be similar in size.

SARDINA KAĦLA; *Sardina pilchardus*, Clupaeidae; *sardina* (It.); *sardine* (Fr.); pilchard. Excellent fried or grilled when fresh, and well known as the tinned sardine.

SARGU; *Diplodus sargus*, Sparidae; *sarago maggiore* (It.); *sar commun* (Fr.); white bream. A truly wonderful fish and much loved in Malta. Bake or grill.

SARGU SKUR; *Diplodus trifasciatus*, Sparidae; *sarago faraone* (It.); *sar à grosses lèvres* (Fr.); three-banded bream. A large fish, it may have more than three bands and has very large lips, hence the French name.

SAWRELLA or SAWRELLA KAĦLA; *Trachurus mediterraneus* or *trachurus*, Carangidae; *suro* or *sugarello* (It.); *saurel (Fr.); scad or horse mackerel. May be cooked in the same way as mackerel and is slightly less oily.*

SAWRELLA IMPERJALI MIBRUMA (also IMPERJALI ĊATTA;) *Caranx fusus* or *kalla* or *Decapterus ronchus*, Carangidae; *carango mediterranea* or *calla* or *carango ronco* (It.); Mediterranean trevally or golden scad.

SAWT; *Trachinus draco*, Trachinidae; *tracna drago* (It.); *grande vive* (Fr.); great weever. Use for *bouillalbaisse,* grill or fry.

SERP; *Ophisurus serpens*, Ophichthidae; *biscia di mare* (It.); serpent-eel.

SERRA; *Lichia amia*, Carangidae; *leccia* (It.); *liche* (Fr.); leer fish. Firm fleshed fish lending itself to a variety of ways of cooking. Bake the large ones.

SERRA TAS-SNIEN; *Pomatomus saltator*, Pomatomidae; *pesce serra* (It.); *tassergal* (Fr.); blue fish. A good fish to grill or cook in the oven wrapped in foil or greaseproof paper with onion, garlic, olive oil and lemon juice.

SILFJUN TAWRU; *Carchiarias ferox* or *taurus*, Squalidae; *caggnaccio squalotoro* (It.); fierce shark or sand shark.

SIRRANA; *Serranus cabrilla*, Serranidae; *perchia* (It.); *serran* (Fr.); comber. All right for soup.

SIRRANA TAR-RAMEL; *Serranus hepatus*, Serranidae; *sacchetto* (It.); *tambour* (Fr.); brown comber.

SKALM; *Synodus saurus*, Synodidae; *pesce ramarro* (It.); lézard (Fr.); lizard fish. Best fried in batter.

SKORFNA SEWDA; Scorpaena porcus, Scorpaenidae; *scorfano nero* (It.); *rascasse noire* (Fr.); small-scale scorpion fish. As all *rascasse*, good for *bouillabaisse*. Large ones may be baked.

SKORFNA TAL-GĦAJN; *Helicolenus dactylopterus*, Scorpaenidae; *scorfano di fondale* (It.); *rascasse de fond* (Fr.); blue mouth. If regarded as a real *rascasse* (a French term) then suitable for *bouillabaisse*, but Davidson regards it as closer lo North Adantic haddock

SKORFNOTT; *Scorpaena notata* or *ustulata*, Scorpaenidae; *scorfanotto* (It.); *petite rascasse* (Fr.); no English term.

SPANJULET; *Aspitriglia obscura* or *Aspitriglia cuculus* or *Trigla pini*, Scorpaenidae; *cappone coccia* or *cappone nero* (It.); *grondin* (Fr.); red gurnard or large-scaled gurnard.

SPARLU; *Diplodus annularis*, Sparidae; *sparaglione* (It.); *sparaillon* (Fr.); annular bream. A small fish. Use for soup.

SPNOTTA; *Dicentrarchus labrax* or *Morone labrax*, Serranidae; *spigola* or *branzino* (It.); *bar* or *loup de mer* (Fr.); bass or sea bass; *qarous* (Tunisian). A very good, firm-fleshed fish which may be cooked whole when large. Small fish may be grilled or baked in foil or greaseproof

SPNOTTA TAT-TBAJJA; *Dicentrarchus punctatus*, Serranidaei; *spigola macchiata* (It.); *bar tacheté (Fr.); black spotted bass; qarous bou nokta* (Tunisian). Cook as above. The names refer to the spots on this fish, although *karus* in Maltese means money-box, and the Tunisian name may also mean bridegroom.

STOKKAFIXX; *Micromesistius poutassou*, Belonidae; *melu* (It.); *poutassou* (Fr.); Couch's whiting or blue whiting. Eat very fresh.

STRAĊNA; *Trachinus vipera*, Trachinidae; *tracina vipera* (It.); *petite vive* (Fr.); lesser weever; *billem zghir* (Tunisian). Have the poisonous spines removed before cooking. Good for bouillabaisse or fried in batter. See also *traċna*.

STRILJA BAGĦLIJA; *Stromateus fiatola*, Stromatidae; *fieto* (It.); *fiatole* (Fr.); pomfret. An unremarkable fish. It may be fried or grilled.

STRIJLA; *Trachynotus glaucus*, Carangidae; *leccia stella* (It.); *palomine* (Fr.); pompano (US name); derbio (early English name). A firm, tunny-like flesh.

STURJUN; *Acipenser*, Acipenseridae; *storione* (It.); *esturgeon* (Fr.); sturgeon. A very rich and meaty fish, often cooked in slices (e.g. like veal), after marinading.

SULTAN IĊ-ĊAWL; *Apogon imberbis*, Apogonidae; *re di triglie* (It.); cardinal fish.

TANNUTA; *Spondyliosoma calitharus*, Sparidae; *tanuta* (It.); *griset* (Fr.); black bream; *kannouta* or *e'houdiya*, meaning 'the Jew' (Tunisian). Not the best of the bream family but still very good.

TIRDA PAGUN (also TIRDA TAL WARDA); *Crenilabrus tinca* or *occelatus*, Labridae; *tordo* (It.); *crénilalbre* (Fr.); wrasse or corkwing; *aroussa* (Tunisian, as in Maltese *għarusa*) or *sultan*. The largest is the peacock wrasse. Basically just good for soups.

TRAĊNA; *Trachinus araneus*, Trachinidae; *tracino ragno* (It.); *vive araignée (Fr.); spotted weever; billem kbir* (Tunisian). See *straċna*.

TRAĊNA TAL-FOND; *Trachinus lineatus*, Trachinidae; *tracina raggiata* or *di fondo* (It.); *vive rayée* (Fr.); streaked weaver. Cook as *traċna* and *straċna*.

TRILJA TAL-ĦAMA; *Mullus barbatus*, Mullidae; *triglia di fango* (It.); *rouget barbet* (Fr.); striped mullet. There are numerous recipes for this and red mullet, below. These are two of the most loved fish in the Mediterranean. May be cooked whole without gutting.

TRILJA TAL-QAWWI; *Mullus surmuletus*, Mullidae; *triglia di scoglio* (It.); *rouget de roche* (Fr.); red mullet. *Qawwi* is Maltese for rough or strong.

TUMBRELL; *Auxit thazard*, Thunnidae; *tombarello* or *biso* (It.); *melva* (Fr.) frigate mackerel; *ebrelli* (Tunisian). Best stewed or braised. Quite a heavy fish.

TUNNAĊĊ: see *kubrita*.

VJOLIN; *Rhinobatus rhinobatus*, Rajidae; *pesce violino* (It.); *guitare* or *violon* (Fr.); guitar fish. A good ray, though not the best.

VOPA; *Boops boops*, Sparidae; *vopa* (It.); *bogue* (Fr.); bogue. A common fish in Malta, but not a great deal can be said for it in culinary terms. The charming Latin description refers to the very large eyes.

WIŻGĦA TAL-BAĦAR (also, possibly, dragunett or FJAMETTA); *Callionymus maculatas* or *lyra*, Callionymidae; *dragoncello macchiato* (It.); common or spotted dragonet.

XABLA; *Lepidopus caudatus*, Trichiuridae; *pesce nastro* or *pesce sciabola* (It.); *sabre* (Fr.); scabbard fish. It is best cut into sections and fried.

XILPA; *Boops salpa*, Sparidae; *salpa* (It.); *saupe* (Fr.); salema. Grilled is best.

XIRGIEN, *Diplodus vulgaris*, Sparidae; *sarago di sabbia* or *fasciato* (It.); *sar doré* (Fr.); two-banded bream. Another delicious member of this family. Tuscans give us some of the best recipes. Always good baked or grilled.

XKATLU; *Squatina squatina* or *Squatina angelus*, Squalidae; *squadro* (It.); *ange de mer* (Fr.); angel shark, angel fish or monkfish. Davidson tells us its dried skin is used by cabinet makers for polishing.

ŻAGĦRUN; *Centrophorus granulosus*, probably Squalidae; *sagri* (It.); rough shark. No other information.

ŻBIRR; *Gobius* (species), Gobiidae; *ghiozzo* (It.); *gobie* (Fr.); goby. Best fried.

ŻIEMEL; *Hippocampus guttulatus*, Syngnathidae; *cavalluccio merino* (It.); seahorse. The Maltese name means horse.

ŻONDU; *Uranoscopus scaber*, Uranoscopidae; *pesce prete* (It.); *boeuf* or *rat* (Fr.); star-gazer. A good fish for soups.

ŻUMBRELL; *Lepidotriglia cavillone*, Triglidae; *caviglone* (It.); large-scaled gurnard. Very small and only useful for soups.

Torta tal-lampuki
Dolphin fish pie

For the pastry
400 g plain flour
200 g butter and lard, mixed, or good margarine
Pinch of salt
4 tbsp (approx.) cold water

For the filling
2 medium sized lampuki *(approx. 400 g)*
1 onion, sliced
2–3 tbsp olive oil
2 large tomatoes, peeled and chopped or 1 dessertspoon tomato purée
1 medium cauliflower
800 g spinach
8 black olives
1 tbsp sultanas
6 walnuts, shelled

see text for traditional alternatives to butter and lard and water.

◆ Make the pastry. Use no more water than necessary. Keep the pastry cold while you prepare the filling.

Cut the fish into 4 or 5 steaks, coat lightly in flour and fry in shallow oil until just cooked. Remove any bones and the skin. Reserve.

In a large pan soften the onion in olive oil . Add the tomatoes, cook for a few minutes more. Add the cauliflower broken into florets and the spinach. Add about 250 ml of boiling water, cover tightly and cook until the vegetables are just tender. Remove from the heat and add the olives, sultanas and walnuts. Season. It is important to let this mixture and the fish get quite cold before finishing the pie.

Line a large shallow pie dish with slightly more than half the pastry. Put half the vegetable mixture over it, then the fish, then the remaining vegetables. Roll out the rest of the pastry to cover. Decorate and brush with beaten egg to which you have added a few drops of oil. Bake at 200°C/400°F/gas 6 for 30 minutes, then at 180°C/350°F/gas 4 until golden brown and the filling heated through. This pie tastes equally good hot or cold.

Some prefer to cook the cauliflower and spinach separately. In this case, add the 250 ml water to the tomato and onion mixture and simmer gently for about half an hour.

It used to be customary to use olive oil instead of butter or other fat to make the pastry, and orange juice instead of water.

A good pie can be made substituting chunks of good quality tinned tuna when *lampaki* are not available. Some cooks use fresh young mackerel, but these are a poor substitute.

We reproduce here a recipe for this pie from

"Il Ctieb tal Chcina" (published in 1908). The name of the dish is given as "Pompa" and we give it in its original Italianate spelling.

"Hu ratal tkiek fin, u keighdu gozz f'nofs ic-cichnatur. F'nofsa ahmel hofra gio gigha titfa dksxein ilma bil melh, aghsar nofs lumia, itfa ucoll isfar ta baida, u ibda aghgen;; meta taghkad zidila imgharfa zeid ftit ftit, uf fl'ahhar cucciarina mastica. Hu pastarda zghira, tmien kattiet spi-naci, sitt klub tal kacocc u nofs artal piselli; ghalli collox ghalieh, hagia hagia, hu lampuca, jew salamunimmellah, jeuinchella salamun tal laned. Il lampuca kattahha roti, xarraba ghal xi quarta uf nofs geuua il hall, erfahha, ixxuttagha u akligha gioz-zejt jaghli. Kalli fiz zeht l'ispanici u il pizelli, itfa mahhom daks tuzzana zebbug, minghair ghadma, uf nors quart zbib sultana. Itfa biccia mill ghagin fil kieh tad-dixx u ibda kieghed ftit minn dac li kalleit. katta il pastarda fiuri fiuri, u kieghed fiur tal pastard, kalba tal kabocc u biccia huta u compli daiiar id-dixx. argia keighed saff spinaci u argia compli bil pastard, kakocc u hut; ghatti collox bil ghagina, aghmila circu tal ghagina max-xifer tad dixx u kieghda fil forn.'

Lampuki biz-zalza pikkanti

Fried dolphin fish in piquant sauce

1 medium lampuka
2–3 tbsp plain flour
Salt and pepper
Piquant sauce (page 217)

◆ Cut the cleaned fish into four steaks. Heat olive oil gently. Dip the pieces of fish in flour and fry them in the hot oil. Test that the fish is cooked through by piercing with a knife to the backbone. There should be no trace of blood. Allow to cool slightly, then remove the bones and place the fish in a shallow dish and season to taste. Pour over the sauce. This dish may be served hot, but definitely tastes better cold.

Lampuki għad-dobbu

Dolphin fish with wine and herbs

2 medium lampuki
(approximately 400 g)
Sprig of rosemary
10 black peppercorns
1 onion, peeled
1 tbsp olive oil
250 ml red wine
Salt to taste

◆ Tie the rosemary and peppercorns in a muslin bag. Put the fish and other ingredients into a saucepan with an extra 125 ml of cold water. Bring to the boil slowly then simmer until the fish is done, approximately 20 minutes.

Lampuki bil-Lumi

Grilled dolphin fish with Lemon

Fillets of fresh lampuki
Butter and olive oil
flour
2 Lemons
Salt and Pepper
Fresh parsley, mint or basil

◆ Coat the lampuki fillets with seasoned flour; fry gently in a mixture of olive oil and butter, turning once. As soon as they are cooked transfer them to a hot dish and keep warm. Squeeze the lemon juice into the frying pan and de-glaze. Pour over the fish and serve at once, sprinkled with the chopped fresh herbs.

Lampuki Tartare

Dolphin Fish Tartare

The fillets from a large freshly caught lampuka weighing about 700 g
1 very finely diced onion
2 crushed cloves of garlic
Coarse sea salt and freshly ground black pepper
Lemon juice
Extra virgin olive oil

◆ We thank Frances Bissell for her permission for us to use this innovative recipe for lampuki "cooked" in a marinade and without heat, which she probably invented in a Gozitan kitchen. The principle is the same as that for the Scandinavian gravadlax and many Japanese raw fish recipes.

Skin the fillets and remove as many of the small bones as possible. This is best done by dividing each fillet in two and removing the line of bones down the centre. Now chop the fish into quite small pieces and mix with the rest of the ingredients, adding salt and pepper gradually. Leave overnight in the refrigerator. Serve with hot toast and lemon wedges.

Imsell mixwi
Grilled Garfish

4 whole garfish
1 lemon
2 tbsp olive oil
1 clove garlic, crushed
2 tbsp chopped parsley
Salt and pepper

◆ Take the garfish and rub the stomach cavities with a halved lemon. Take hold of each snout and press it into the skin immediately above the tail, thus forming a circle. Mix the oil, juice of half a lemon, garlic, parsley and seasoning and spread this mixture over the fish. Cook, under a preheated hot grill for 10–15 minutes, basting frequently. Reduce the heat after the first 5 minutes and serve immediately. Charcoal grilling produces the best flavour.

Gandoffli jew tamar tal-baħar fil-forn
Baked warty Venus

Gandoffli
Fresh white bread crumbs
Chopped parsley
Garlic
Grated lemon rind
Lemon juic e
Olive oil, salt and pepper
Galletti *crumbs*

◆ The English name for this mollusc is warty Venus. This may sound exotic, but it is no probably more familiar to us as the French *praire*. *Tamar tal-baħar* means 'sea dates'. They may be eaten raw, but remember pollution. In this recipe, they are cooked in the oven, in a way similar to stuffed mussels. Before eating or preparing them for cooking, leave them for a while in water so that they can release any sand they contain.

Open the *gandoffli* and remove their contents. Keep the shells. Chop the flesh very small and mix with the bread crumbs, garlic and parsley mixture, together with the grated lemon rind and the juice. The quantities will depend on the amount of shells you have. Season with salt and pepper and fill the half shells with the mixture. Place them close together in a shallow fireproof oven dish which you have greased lightly with olive oil. Sprinkle with olive oil and some *galletti* crumbs – not too much. Add a tablespoonful or two of water to the bottom of the dish. Cook uncovered at 200°C/400°C/gas 6 for 15–20 minutes.

Sfineċ tal-inċova
Anchovy puffs

For the batter
200 g plain flour
1 level tsp baking powder
Salt
250 ml water
100 g anchovy fillets

◆ Sieve the flour and baking powder and add enough water to give a hard, dropping consistency. Knead briefly. Allow to stand for at least an hour, preferably two. Divide each anchovy fillet into two, dip into the batter and fry until golden in deep oil. Serve very hot. For a lighter batter add a teaspoonful of olive oil and, just before using, fold in the stiffly beaten white of one egg.

Ċerna biz-salza pikkanti
Grouper with piquant sauce

Half a lemon
A few black peppercorns
Salt and pepper
1 good sized grouper

◆ Bring enough water to cover the fish to the boil with all the ingredients except the fish. Lower the heat as much as possible and slip the fish in. Poach gently until cooked. As always, the timing depends on the size of the fish. Serve with piquant sauce (see page 217). You might prefer to cook the grouper in foil as in the dentex recipe.

Fritturi tal-makku
Pellucid sole (or transparent goby) fritters

400 g makku
2 beaten eggs
Deep oil for frying

◆ This is one of the simplest and best fish recipes. The fish is tiny, similar to whitebait. In Gozo they are known as *nemusa*, mosquitoes. They need no cleaning and the whole fish is eaten, including the head. Rinse the fish well in a colander and dry on kitchen paper. Taking a few fish at a time, dip them into the beaten egg and deep fry until golden brown. Drain on kitchen paper and keep warm until all the fish has been cooked. Serve very hot with lemon wedges. Some cooks like to beat the egg white separately and add to the beaten yolk just before dipping the fish.

Bebbux biz-zalza ħadra
Snails with green sauce

8–12 snails per person

◆ Keep the snails under a large flower pot, out of doors, for about 2 days. Wash them thoroughly in salted water. Place in a large pan with water to cover and boil for about 15 minutes When cooked the snail can be easily removed from the shell using a skewer. If it does not come free, further cooking is required. Discard any black threads. Serve cold with the green sauce (page 218). Green sauce sounds uninspiring, but try it. Provided you like garlic you will love this sauce.

Stuffat tal-bebbux
Snail stew

◆ Prepare the snails in the same way as in the recipe above. When cooked remove the snails from the shell and finish cooking them in a good tomato sauce for another half hour or so.

Stuffat tal-bakkaljaw
Salt Cod Stew

600 g salt cod
Slice of lemon
2 sliced onions
2 cloves of garlic, chopped
2 tbsp olive oil
2 tbsp tomato purée
1 medium cauliflower, in florets
300 g pumpkin, chopped
600 g potatoes, peeled and quartered
8 stoned and chopped black olives
1 tbsp chopped fresh mint
Half tsp felfel

◆ Soak the salt cod for several hours, with a slice of lemon, changing the water frequently.

Fry the onions lightly in the oil, add first the garlic, then the tomato paste and the fish, cut into pieces. Add the vegetables, then the olives and enough water to cover. Cover and cook on a slow flame until the vegetables are tender. Do not add salt as the cod is salty enough. Finish with the mint and the *felfel* and check for seasoning.

Felfel is a very hot pickle – it can usually be obtained outside the Valletta market, or at the entrance to Valletta, where you can also buy capers, fresh herbs, rocket and other fresh produce. If you cannot get *felfel* use the same amount of hot dried red chili peppers. When buying salt cod, go for small fish – large ones tend to be stringy.

Sfineċ tal-bakkaljaw

Salt cod fritters

400 g salt cod
150 g plain flour
1 tsp baking powder
A pinch of salt
A squeeze of lemon juice
2 peeled and chopped tomatoes, seeds removed
1 or 2 cloves of garlic, crushed

◆ Soak the cod in cold water for several hours, discarding and replacing the water several times. Make the batter as in the recipe for anchovy puffs above and add the lemon juice. Allow it to stand for at least an hour. Boil the fish until tender, cut into strips when cold and stir into the batter with the tomatoes and crushed garlic. Fry as small balls until golden brown in deep oil. Drain well and serve hot.

Stuffat tal-qarnit

Octopus Stew

1 octopus of 600–800 g
2 tbsp olive oil
4 large onions, chopped
2 tbsp tomato purée
8 olives
1 tbsp capers
1 tbsp chopped fresh mint
1 tsp each mixed spice and curry powder
A handful each of walnuts and sultanas
250 ml red wine
Salt and pepper

◆ Do not be put off by the slimy and unattractive appearance of uncooked octopus. Ask the fishmonger to remove the ink sac and the eyes. Wash under running water and beat it well with a meat hammer. Skin it, then cut it with a sharp knife into bite-sized pieces.

Heat the oil and fry the onion in it until golden. Add the octopus and cook slowly for a few minutes. Add all the other ingredients, cover and simmer gently for an hour, then remove the lid and continue simmering for another hour, stirring from time to time. Do not allow to boil nor to become dry. If necessary, add a little hot water.

The stew may be served piping hot over spaghetti or as a main course by adding 600 g of peeled and quartered potatoes for the last hour of the cooking time. Make sure there is enough liquid in the pan to see the potatoes through until they are cooked. The addition of curry powder and spice may sound outrageous, but is a typically Maltese addition which must have emerged during the reign of the British, who at the time were running a thriving trade in spices around the world.

Stuffat tal-fekruna
Turtle stew

◆ We have deleted this recipe because turtles are now an endangered species.

Insalata tal-qarnit
Octopus salad

800 g octopus
6 tbsp olive oil
4 cloves garlic, crushed
1 bunch fresh parsley, chopped
Juice of at least 1 lemon
Salt and pepper

◆ If the octopus is very large you will want to remove the outer skin, but this is not necessary in a young octopus. Ensure it is well beaten and tender. Stew in salted water until tender, approximately 1 hour. A pressure cooker will decrease the time considerably. Drain; mix with the olive oil. Allow to cool and slice into thin pieces. Mix with the other ingredients. Eat cold.

Tunnaċċ jew tonn fil-forn
Baked blue-fin tuna cutlets

4 fresh tuna cutlets
4 tbsp olive oil
Juice of a lemon
1–2 cloves of garlic, crushed
2 tbsp finely chopped parsley
Salt and pepper

◆ Marinate the fish in a mixture of the olive oil, lemon juice and crushed garlic. Lift the slices into a shallow, oven-proof dish, pouring the marinade over them. Sprinkle with the parsley, salt and pepper. Bake at 180°C/350°F/gas 4 for 20–30 minutes, basting once. A lovely creamy coloured sauce will form over the fish. Serve at once, with sauté or chipped potatoes.

Tunnaċċ jew tonn mixwi
Grilled blue-fin tuna

4 large fresh tuna cutlets
2 tbsp fresh white bread crumbs
2 crushed cloves of garlic
2 tbsp finely chopped parsley
Salt and pepper
2 tbsp olive oil

◆ Spread the fish with a mixture of the bread crumbs, garlic, parsley, salt and pepper. Pour over the olive oil. Cook under a hot grill for approximately 5 minutes on each side.

Stuffat tat-tonn taż-żejt
Tinned tuna fish stew

Potatoes, onions and garlic as for patata fgata *(page 162)*
500 g ripe tomatoes, peeled and chopped
1 tsp sugar
Salt and pepper
200 g tin of tuna in brine, drained
Handful of capers, drained
Chopped fresh parsley, mint or basil
1–2 tbsp olive oil

◆ This is the simplest of recipes, useful because it can be made with ingredients most of us always have in the house. It was passed on to us by the grand-daughter of Mrs Milanes.

Chop potatoes, onions and garlic as for *patata fgata* and place in a heavy saucepan. Pour over the tomatoes. Add a little water if the potatoes are not quite covered. Add the sugar, salt and pepper, bring to the boil, cover and simmer gently until the potatoes are cooked. Add the drained tuna to the stew with the olives and capers, the herbs and the olive oil. Alternatively you may omit the olive oil and use a tin of tuna in olive oil – other kinds of oil will diminish the flavour. Eat hot with crusty bread, a green vegetable or salad. You may like to add a few chopped walnuts and sultanas.

Dentiċi bil-mayonnaise
Dentex with mayonnaise

Half a lemon
Salt
Black peppercorns
A few parsley stalks
A dentex weighing 1.5 kg

◆ You will need a fish kettle big enough to hold the whole fish.

Prepare a *court bouillon* by bringing enough water to cover the fish to the boil with the lemon, salt, peppercorns and parsley stalks.

Slip in the fish carefully, and poach gently for 20–30 minutes. Lift out gingerly and serve as soon as possible with mayonnaise.

An alternative way is to cook dentex or other large, delicate fish in foil in the oven. This method is described at the beginning of this chapter, on page 44.

Pixxispad mixwi
Grilled swordfish

4 tbsp olive oil
Juice of a lemon
2 cloves of garlic, crushed
4 tbsp finely chopped parsley
Salt and pepper
4 swordfish cutlets or steaks (12 mm thick)

◆ Mix the oil, lemon juice, garlic, parsley and seasoning. Pour over the fish. Cook under a moderate grill, basting frequently, turning the fish over once. It should cook in about 10–15 minutes, depending on the thickness of the cutlets.

Frozen fish does not have the same texture or flavour as fresh.

Swordfish steaks can also be coated lightly in seasoned flour and fried in olive oil for 7 to 8 minutes, turning once.

Klamari mimlijin
Stuffed cuttlefish

700–800 g fresh cuttlefish
2 tbsp olive oil
2 finely chopped onions
4 large tomatoes, peeled, seeded and chopped
200 g fresh white bread crumbs
1 hard-boiled egg, chopped
1 tbsp capers
2 finely chopped olives
1 fillet anchovy
1 tbsp fresh mixed herbs, such as parsley, thyme and marjoram
1 beaten egg

◆ To clean the cuttlefish, hold the body in one hand, and with the other pull the head out gently. Discard the insides, but keep the tentacles. Remove the cartilage from the tubelike body. Rinse under cold running water. Some people beat the flesh with a wooden spoon to tenderise it.

Heat the oil and fry the onion lightly. Add the tomatoes and cook gently for about half an hour. Remove 2 tbsp of this sauce to moisten the ingredients of the filling. Add the reserved sauce to the bread crumbs, hard-boiled egg, the capers, olives, anchovy, herbs and the beaten raw egg and mix well. Fill the cuttlefish with this mixture and secure the open end with a thread or a cocktail stick. Add to the hot tomato sauce and simmer until cooked, about 45 minutes. Add a little liquid to the sauce if it gets too dry.

The sauce is usually served with spaghetti. The fish may be cut into rings and served at the same time, or may be served separately

❖❖❖❖❖

The following three recipes from Sir Harry Luke's "The Tenth Muse" are included to give an idea of how the British Governors' chefs used to present the best fish and crustacea.

Eating should be a pleasure to the eyes as well as to the palate, but some would sacrifice the second entirely for the first. This is one way to prepare a dentici but also a good way of detracting from the exquisite flavour of such a fine fish. It is also likely to be overcooked. It was passed on to Sir Harry by the wife of a governor and described as a favourite Maltese (sic) dish for a spring or summer luncheon party.

Dentici Froid aux Rubis

◆ Take a good sized dentice (around 5 lbs) and boil in a court-bouillon for 6 minutes to each pound, wrapping the fish in a muslin to keep it together. Then simmer for half an hour and when cold, skin and bone the fish and re-form on a napkin, the head and tail being retained in place. Now cover the fish with chopped red aspic made from the court bouillon and garnish the dish with stuffed eggs, prawns, diced cucumber and tomatoes. Serve with a mayonnaise, Remoulade or Green Sauce.

Shellfish and Crustacea

1 medium sized lobster
1 glass sherry
1 tin black mushrooms (did this mean truffles?)
1 tin champignons
Lobster stock, prepared from the shell
3 egg yolks
4 fresh tomatoes
cayenne, salt and pepper
1 tin cream
lemon juice

◆ To the best of our knowledge there are no specifically Maltese ways with lobster and other shellfish. Readers please correct us if we are wrong. Lobster is generally prepared very simply or according to one of the international recipes such as Thermidor or Newburg. Sir Harry Luke gives this recipe created in the kitchens of the Union Club. Clearly devised at a time when fresh cream and mushrooms were unavailable, you might like to try this now that they are. We have not tried the recipe but, with fresh ingredients, it promises to be good. We give it just as it appears in The Tenth Muse

◆ Cook the lobster. When perfectly cold, open and put the flesh into a casserole, together with the other ingredients and cook in the oven for about 20 minutes.

Sir Harry comments 'An exceedingly succulent and not too complicated lobster dish.'

Lobster Cocktail

◆ This came from Governor Sir John du Cane's Polish cook at San Anton Palace (c 1927 to 31)

Make an Hollandaise sauce with three eggs mixed with one tablespoon Heinz tomato sauce, one tablespoon Worcester Sauce, 1 glass brandy and Tabasco pepper. Mix small pieces of cold, boiled lobster with the sauce and serve cold in champagne glasses.

LAĦAM
MEAT DISHES

'Maltese meat is the best I ever tasted out of England, and bears a higher price than that which is imported'

W. I. Monson, Extracts from a Journal 1820.

Some things change yet stay the same, others really change. The marketing and consumption of meat has changed and continues to do so in our islands as in other parts of Europe.

There are two main reasons for change; the advent of large supermarkets which threaten the livelihood of the small traditional butchers, and growing awareness of health issues amongst the general population. It is strange that some dangers to health grip the imagination, for example that chicken and fish are healthier than red meats, while others, like the dangers of too much sugar and fat in the diet, are ignored. Witness the over-consumption of sweet drinks and confectionery.

In reaction to competition from supermarket styles of packaging, and a desire to appear 'modern' in our shopping habits, individual butchers are buying smaller quantities of meat and selling it as quickly as possible, so that it is hardly being hung at all. Flavour and texture are adversely affected. The changes are surreptitious, one hardly notices them if one visits the Valletta market or butchers' shops in the villages and it is possible that both butchers themselves and the public will recognize that change is not always for the better. Women who work outside the home can no longer afford to spend hours queuing at the butchers. Women who are fully employed in the home (but are unpaid) do still spend long periods of time in shop queues and, because many butchers and greengrocers operate single-handed, one can wait a very long time to get served. But shops and shopping have remained potent forces for social interaction, something which has been lost in large lonely European cities.

What of the meat itself? Certainly there is not much sign yet of a reduction in consumption. The older generation complains that meat no longer tastes as good as it used to in the days of their youth or 'before the War', yet young people in their twenties who have gone to live abroad also insist the meat in Malta tastes better than anywhere else.

Minced beef and pork seems to have a better texture and flavour and the butchers are accustomed to mincing it on the spot (hence more waiting time). In our first edition we described the baking tray of meat and potatoes, covered with a cloth and taken to the baker's oven: the joint of pork or other meat, lying on a bed of halved potatoes and onions, sprinkled with sea salt and black pepper. This custom has not died out, since many believe that roasting in the public oven produces a better result than when it is cooked at home. So the old tradition continues, with the numbered metal disc placed on each customer's dish.

Perhaps the most characteristically Maltese meat is the rabbit. This little animal has had significance thrust upon it from the most unlikely quarters. Introduced into England by the conquering Normans and symbol of one aspect of feudal repression, it was to have much the same significance to the Maltese peasantry, who were denied rabbits by their hunting-mad masters the Knights, yet suffered from their assaults on their crops. The anthropologist Carmel Cassar has discussed this in his book Fenkata, an Emblem of Maltese Peasant Resistance. "Cassar (pages 19–20) sites evidence from Mastro Vincentio Azupard that our "fenkata" was not the traditional way of eating rabbit, rather that it was pre-dated by rabbit pies.

Cassar's work is highly recommended and includes delightful accounts of people who indulged in meat-eating both during Lent and on other lean days when the eating of meat, cheese and eggs was prohibited by the Church. Fenkata has now become the national dish and is thus in danger of becoming cheapened as it is promoted on tourist menus, though this need not be its fate. A Fenkata today is best described as a kind of rabbit outing or celebration where a family or group of friends goes out into the country to eat a dish of spaghetti and rabbit.

Cassar (p25) suggests that such feasts, and the taste for rabbit may have been 'deliberately chosen to characterise one of the ways in which the Maltese differed from the Knights.' at a time when even the Maltese elite treated the latter with polite disdain.'

One of the most important of these gatherings took place at Buskett, near the cathedral of Mdina, on the night of the feast of St Peter and St Paul (June 29th) called the *Mnarja* (from the Italian *luminarja*, 'illumination'). It was the profane celebration of midsummer, as High Mass in the cathedral was the sacred. Groups would drink, cook rabbit, sing folksongs, and dance away the night. It is not so long ago but that people recall marriage contracts stipulating that the husband must take his intended wife to this festival.

At first, we were loath to include any of the game recipes that were part of the first edition of this book. Wildfowl have been hunted enough in Malta, and we did not wish to be party to more destruction. However, many of the birds we termed game are available outside the islands as domesticated or farmed meats, and inclusion of the recipe here does not constitute a licence to kill innocent migrants.

Falda mimlija
Stuffed flank

1 kg beef flank
4–6 tbsp fresh bread crumbs
300 g minced pork
100 g chopped ham or bacon
1 tbsp finely chopped onion
1 hard-boiled egg, chopped
3 eggs
2 tsp grated Parmesan
Salt and pepper

◆ Ask the butcher to prepare an opening in the flank. Combine all the remaining ingredients and stuff the flank, then sew up the opening. Place the meat in a saucepan of boiling water and add the same chopped vegetables as in *brodu tal-laħam* (page 32). Simmer very slowly for about 2½ hours.

Prepare a thick onion, carrot and tomato sauce; remove the flank from the soup and pour over the hot sauce. Serve with boiled or mashed potatoes and a green vegetable.

Bragoli
Beef olives

8 slices topside (about 800 g) sliced thinly as for schnitzel

For the stuffing
6 rashers streaky bacon
2 hard-boiled eggs, chopped
2 tbsp finely chopped parsley
4 tbsp fresh bread crumbs
Salt and pepper
2 cloves garlic, crushed

For the sauce
2 large onions, sliced
2 tbsp olive oil
2 cloves garlic, crushed
1 bay leaf
150 ml red wine

◆ Trim the meat, removing any fat, and beat it on both sides with a meat hammer. Prepare the stuffing by chopping the bacon finely and adding it to the other ingredients. Lay out the slices of beef. Place I tbsp or a little more of the stuffing on each slice, leaving one third uncovered. Roll up from the covered end and secure with string or toothpicks. Fry the olives in shallow oil until brown all over. Remove to a plate. In the same pan fry the onions and garlic in more oil until golden brown, return the meat to the pan and cook everything together on a low heat. Add the bay leaf and the wine. Cover and simmer for about I hour. Add extra stock or water to stop it drying out.

Some cooks add tomato purée to the onions. Another variation is to fry chopped or ringed carrots with the onions and add a cup of cooked fresh peas at the end. Some like to roll the *bragoli* in seasoned flour before frying. This serves to thicken the sauce but the result can be achieved by getting the liquid to the right consistency by slow and careful cooking.

Bragoli mixwijin
Grilled beef olives

The same amount of beef and the same stuffing ingredients as in the previous recipe
8 bay leaves
8 pieces of caul – mindil

◆ Make the *bragoli* in the same way as in the recipe above, then wrap each one in caul with a bay leaf tucked inside. Thread on skewers. These taste best if grilled on charcoal but otherwise, cook fairly slowly under a moderate grill, turning frequently. Cooking time will depend on the tenderness of the meat.

Other variations of this dish are to marinade the meat in wine, oil and herbs for several hours, or to use thin slices of liver (pig's liver would be most popular in Malta) instead of the beef, and to proceed in either of the ways described above.

Braġolun
A single beef olive

1 kg topside of beef in one piece
The same stuffing as for braġoli
A piece of caul
Sauce as for braġoli

◆ Ask the butcher to cut open the meat to make one large flat piece suitable for stuffing and rolling. It should be approximately 10 mm thick. Beat it well to flatten it. Prepare the stuffing and lay it out over the meat. Roll it up and wrap it in the caul or tie it securely with string.

The meat may now be roasted. Calculate the time as for roast beef and start it at 200°C/400°F/gas 6, reducing the heat after the first 15 minutes or so. Alternatively, braise in the same way as the first version of beef olives. Serve hot, thickly sliced, and accompanied by roast or mashed potatoes and with a green vegetable or salad to follow.

Laħam fuq il-fwar
Steamed beef

The same ingredients as for braġoli

◆ Bearing in mind that the traditional Maltese meal frequently begins with soup, this must have been devised as an energy-saving way of using the steam from the soup pan.

Trim and prepare the meat as in the *braġoli* recipe. Grease a casserole with butter or olive oil. Layer the slices of meat and stuffing and season well with pepper. Salt is added when the meat is cooked. Cover with greased greaseproof paper or foil and steam over soup or a pan of steadily simmering water for a good 2 hours. The dish can also be cooked in a covered casserole in a moderate oven.

Another variation was brought to our attention from someone in New Zealand. Instead of layers made with thin slices of beef simply cut thick slices into cubes, mix it together with the stuffing and steam in the same way. Serve with potatoes.

Buljut
Boiled beef

◆ The rather shrunken piece of shin of beef which has been used to make the broth described in the chapter on soup may not seem very appetising, but provided it has not been allowed to boil fiercely and become overcooked, it makes an excellent second course.

Cut into neat pieces and place on a hot dish surrounded by freshly boiled potatoes, sprinkled with chopped parsley. Serve hot with a green sauce (page 218), which may be spread over the meat or served separately. A little olive oil may be poured over the meat for a delicious flavour. *Buljut* may also be used to make meat balls (page 97), or for *ravjuletti tal-laħam* (page 93).

Ċanga bil-patata fil-forn
Malta roast beef

2 kg roasting joint
1 kg large potatoes
3–4 onions
Rock salt and black pepper
Fresh or dried thyme
2 cloves garlic, crushed
1 bay leaf
2–3 tbsp olive oil
250 ml stock or water

◆ Weigh the meat and calculate the cooking time, allowing 20 minutes per 400 g for a very thick joint, or 15 minutes per 400 g if the joint is not very deep. These timings are for rare to medium, with the oven at 200°C/400°F/gas 6.

Peel the potatoes and onions, cut the potatoes horizontally into 2 or 3 slices. Slice the onions and layer the potatoes and onions in a large baking dish, lightly greased. Sprinkle with rock salt and pepper, the herbs and the crushed garlic. Lay the meat on top and pour on more oil and seasoning. Tuck the bay leaf underneath the joint. Pour over the water or stock and place in the oven. Turn the potatoes and onions over once or twice during cooking to ensure that the onions do not burn. When cooked the potatoes and onions will not be browned in the English style but moist and flavoursome because of the liquid that has been added. Should you have only a small joint of meat, start the potatoes and onions half an hour or so earlier so that meat and potatoes will be ready at the same time.

Ilsien biz-zalza tad-tadam

Fresh ox tongue with tomato sauce

1 fresh ox tongue (not pickled)
2 carrots, chopped
2 onions, chopped
1 kohl rabi, chopped
1 stick of celery, chopped
Salt and black peppercorns

For the sauce
1 tbsp olive oil
1 medium onion, chopped
2–3 tbsp tomato purée
375 ml stock or water
½ cup of fresh cooked peas

◆ Wash the tongue well and remove any fatty pieces. Place in a deep pot with the chopped vegetables, salt and peppercorns, and enough boiling water to cover. Simmer very slowly for about 3 hours. The tongue must be skinned while it is hot. Remove any remaining fat.

Sweat the onion for the sauce in olive oil. Add the tomato purée, and stock or water. Simmer for 45 minutes. Add the cooked peas. Slice the tongue and heat it in the sauce. A piquant sauce also makes an excellent accompaniment (page 217)

Ilsien għad-dobbu

Braised ox tongue with wine and herbs

1 ox tongue (not pickled)
2 rashers unsmoked bacon
2 onions stuck with cloves
2 carrots, chopped
2 whole sprigs parsley
3 sprigs fresh rosemary
1 bay leaf
8 black peppercorns
375 ml red wine
Parsley to garnish
Grated lemon rind

◆ Prepare the tongue as in the recipe above. Make small incisions with a sharp knife or skewer and insert pieces of bacon evenly through the tongue. Tie the tongue into a round and place it in a large pot with all the remaining ingredients. Cover it with cold water. Simmer gently, covered. When cooked it will feel tender. Test with a skewer. Skin the tongue while it is hot. Reserve.

Strain the liquid and reduce it by half. Cool and refrigerate. It will set overnight. Lift the fat from the top, slice the tongue and serve the jelly with it . Dress it liberally with chopped parsley and freshly grated lemon rind.

Ravjuletti tal-laħam

Little meat pies

For the filling
1 onion, finely chopped
2 tbsp olive oil
1 rasher bacon, chopped
300 g lean beef mince
2 tsp tomato purée
1 tbsp finely chopped parsley

For the pastry
400 g plain flour
200 g butter
Pinch of salt
5 tbsp cold water

◆ Fry the chopped onion in the olive oil, add the bacon then the mince. It is possible to use cooked beef which can be minced at home. In this case it would be added at the end of the preparation. Add the tomato puree and cook until well absorbed then add the parsley. The mixture must be dry.

Make the pastry as for shortcrust. Roll it out, using one half at a time. Shape into a strip 10 cm wide. Put teaspoonfuls of the meat mixture down one side. Wet the edge and fold over, pressing down well between each pocket. Cut into semicircles using a pastry wheel. Heat deep oil, and fry a few at a time until golden brown. Take care not to let them brown too quickly. Dry off on kitchen paper and serve very hot.

Pastizz tal-laħam

Large meat pie

200 g potatoes
Puff or flaky pastry (made with 200 g flour)
400 g rump steak, beaten flat and cut in strips
2 spring onions or young leeks, chopped
2 hard-boiled eggs, chopped
2 rashers streaky bacon
125 ml stock
Salt and pepper
Beaten egg to glaze

◆ Peel the potatoes and slice them thinly. Use half the pastry to line a greased pie dish. Arrange the potato slices over the pastry. Place about half the meat over the potatoes, season it, then sprinkle with spring onions, hardboiled eggs and bacon. Finish with a layer of the remainder of the meat. Pour over a little stock. Season and cover with the remaining pastry. Crimp the edges and decorate the top then brush with beaten egg. Bake at 400°C/200°F/gas 6 for 45 minutes. Reduce to 180°C/350°F/gas 4 and continue cooking for 30 minutes. Serve hot. It can also be eaten cold with a salad.

Luċertu bbutunat

Larded silverside

2.5 kg fresh silverside of beef
8 long strips of bacon
1 tbsp chopped parsley
2 cloves garlic, crushed
2 tbsp olive oil
2 onions, sliced
250 ml red wine
250 ml stock
6 carrots, sliced
100 g fresh peas, weighed when podded

◆ Pierce the joint from end to end with a sharp poultry knife so that you have three or four holes in it. Lard these all the way through with the strips of bacon, the parsley and the garlic. Heat the oil and brown the meat gently on all sides. Reserve while you fry the sliced onions for a further 5 or 10 minutes. Return the meat to the pan and add the wine, bring to a simmer then add the stock (or water). Simmer, covered, until the beef is cooked (about 2½ hours). In the last 45 minutes, add the sliced carrots. Add the peas for the last 15 minutes. Slice the meat thickly and serve with boiled potatoes and the juices in the pan. The joint may also be roasted for approximately 1¼ hours in a moderate oven.

Laħam bil-panura
Beef schnitzel

4 thin slices of rump steak
Seasoned flour
1 tbsp finely chopped parsley
Salt and pepper
1 beaten egg
1 cup fresh bread crumbs
Olive oil for frying
Lemon quarters

◆ The beef should be sliced twice as thick as for veal schnitzel. Coat the slices with seasoned flour. Add the chopped parsley and salt and pepper to the beaten egg and dip each slice of meat in this, then coat well with the bread crumbs, pressing them into the meat, using very clean hands. Ensure the crumbs cover the entire slice of meat. Some cooks repeat the process for good measure.

Heat the olive oil and fry the slices of beef for 5 minutes, turning once. Clean the pan and start afresh for each steak unless you can fit all the slices at once. Serve with lemon quarters, creamed potatoes, tomato sauce and a green vegetable or salad. Thin slices of tender pork may be cooked in the same way but will require longer cooking. Start with a high heat for the first minute, then reduce considerably. Turn the slices over, start with a high heat again, then reduce.

Ċanga bit-tewma
Garlic-flavoured steak

4 slices of rump or sirloin approximately 6 cm thick
2–3 tbsp olive oil
Ground black pepper
Juice of 1 lemon
4–6 large cloves of garlic, crushed
1 tbsp wine vinegar
Salt and pepper

◆ Marinade the meat in a deep dish, pouring the lemon juice and 2 tbsp oil and pepper over it. Leave for several hours.

Drain off the marinade and fry the slices of meat. Make sure the oil is very hot and fry the beef quickly until brown on each side. When all the meat has been cooked, add the garlic to the pan and cook lightly, without browning, for a few seconds. De-glaze the pan with the vinegar, and pour this sauce over the meat. Season well with salt and pepper.

Laħam fis-seffud
Grilled beef on skewers

400 g rump steak, cubed
4–6 slices white bread, in cubes
2–3 rashers streaky bacon
Bay leaves

Marinade
2 tbsp olive oil, lemon juice, crushed garlic and pepper

◆ Marinade the meat for several hours or overnight. Thread four skewers with alternate pieces of beef, bread, bacon and bay leaf Brush with more olive oil and cook on a very hot grill (charcoal is ideal) for 10 minutes or so, turning frequently.

Majjal fil-forn
Maltese roast pork

◆ This is made in the same way as roast beef (page 87) but you should allow 30–35 minutes per 400 g and 30 minutes extra, at 200°C/400°F/gas 6. Pork should not be served undercooked. Place the sliced onions between 2 layers of potatoes. Make sure that the oil and water do not dry out. Turn the potatoes and onions over from time to time.

Pulpetti
Meat balls

1 large onion, finely chopped
1 tbsp olive oil
1–2 cloves garlic, crushed
1 tsp tomato purée
2 rashers streaky bacon, chopped
1 egg
1 tbsp parsley, chopped
400 g minced meat
½ cup fresh breadcrumbs
Salt and pepper
Flour or semolina
Olive oil for frying

◆ Pulpetti are often made with the remains of cooked meat, but are greatly improved by the addition of fresh minced pork.

Fry the chopped onion in olive oil until soft. Add the garlic and the tomato purée, mixed with 125 ml cold water. Cook together until reduced to a thick puree. Mix this with all the other ingredients and season to taste with salt and pepper. Roll the mixture into small balls, each the size of a large walnut. Roll in plain flour or semolina and fry in olive oil. Cook slowly and thoroughly if you have included fresh pork in the mixture. If you have used only cooked meat it is just a matter of heating the meat balls through and browning them. Serve with lemon wedges and fried potatoes or with pasta and tomato sauce.

Pastizzoti tal-laħam
Small meat pies

Puff pastry (made with 200 g flour)
The meat mixture described above made with cooked minced meat
Beaten egg to glaze

◆ Lightly grease a tray of tartlet tins and line each one with pastry. Fill them with the pulpetti mixture, wet the edges of the pastry and cover each tartlet with a lid or with strips of pastry then glaze with beaten egg. Bake at 425°C/220°F/gas 7 for 10–15 minutes. Serve very hot.

Torta tal-kappuljat
Large meat pie

1 onion, chopped
2 tbsp olive oil
2 rashers streaky bacon
350 g minced beef
350 g minced pork
2 tsp tomato purée
100 g fresh peas, cooked
3 eggs, beaten
Salt and pepper
Puff pastry (made with 200 g flour)
2 hard-boiled eggs, sliced
400 g spinach, cooked
Pinch of mixed spice
2 tbsp grated Parmesan

◆ Fry the onions in the olive oil, add the bacon and the minced pork. Cook for 15 minutes then add the beef and tomato purée. Stir well until the meat turns golden brown, then lower the heat and allow to simmer until the meat is thoroughly cooked. Stir in the peas. Cool the mixture and add the beaten eggs and seasoning, reserving a little beaten egg for glazing the pastry. Roll out half the pastry and use it to line a greased oven-proof dish. Spoon in the cold meat mixture and the sliced hard-boiled eggs. Place a layer of spinach on top then cover with the other half of the pastry, remembering to wet the edges and to seal them together. Decorate with pastry leaves and glaze with beaten egg. Bake at 200°C/400°F/gas 6 for 15–20 minutes, then at 190°C/375°F/gas 5 for a further 20 minutes, until golden brown.

Majjal fgat
Smothered pork

800 g–1 kg cross section of the leg of pork, about 5 cm thick
2–3 tbsp fresh bread crumbs
1 tbsp olive oil
1 tbsp chopped parsley
1–2 cloves garlic
Salt and pepper

◆ Heat the oil in a heavy saucepan and place the pork in it. Cover the joint with all the other ingredients. Cover with a tight-fitting lid and cook very gently, allowing 30 minutes per 400 g. When the pork fat starts to melt, use it to baste the meat. Some cooks like to add the juice of half a lemon. The dish may also be cooked covered in a moderate to hot oven, but you would still need to brown the meat to begin. This may be eaten hot or cold with appropriate vegetables

Ilsna tal-majjal
Pork tongues

◆ Pork tongues are smaller and more delicate in taste than ox-tongues. They also cook more quickly. Prepare and serve in the same way as braised ox tongue with wine and herbs (page 93). Cook them a day before you need them to let the fat rise to the surface of the liquid. This can be easily removed.

In hot weather the soup may be made into a jelly. Use 12 g of powdered gelatine to each 500 ml stock, following the makers' instructions. When the gelatine has dissolved, pour it from a height into the hot stock, stirring gently but thoroughly. You may add white wine or dry sherry. Pack the cooked tongues to fit snugly into a round dish. Pour the hot stock over them then allow to cool before refrigerating until set. This may take several hours. Remove any fat which has formed on the surface, turn the tongues on to an attractive dish, sprinkle with fresh chopped parsley and serve with salad and bread or potatoes.

Torta tal-majjal bil-qara aħmar

Gozitan pork and pumpkin pie

400 g long grain rice
2 tbsp olive oil
1 large onion sliced
2 cloves of garlic, crushed
400 g minced pork
800 g pumpkin, peeled and diced
Puff pastry (made with 200 g flour)

◆ Gozo is the second largest island in the Maltese archipelago. Gozitans are extremely fond of pies and this is just one example.

Boil the rice in salted water until just done. Make sure not to overcook as the whole dish will suffer. Drain and leave to cool.

Fry the onion until golden, add the garlic, then the pork and continue until it is slightly coloured. Add the pumpkin, in small dice. Stir well together, cover and simmer until both pumpkin and pork are cooked. You may need to add a little water or wine to prevent sticking. Allow to cool then mix with the cooked rice and check for seasoning.

Roll out half the pastry and use this to line a lightly greased shallow pie dish. Spoon in the cold mixture, wet the edges of the pastry and cover with a lid rolled from the remainder of the pastry. Bake for 15 minutes at 220°C/425°F/gas 7; finish at 180°C/350°F/gas 4 until the pastry is golden. Serve hot with a green vegetable or a salad.

Majjal għad-dobbu
Pork en daube

1.25–1.5 kg leg of pork
1 pig's trotter or 2 medium-sized bones
2 large onions stuck with a few cloves
2 carrots
2 sprigs parsley
3 sprigs rosemary
2 bay leaves
8 peppercorns
375–500 ml red wine
250 ml water
Salt

◆ We believe this dish takes its Maltese name from the French 'en daube'.

Ask the butcher to give you a cut from the middle of the leg so as to have a compact joint. Place all the ingredients in a large saucepan. Bring to the boil, cover and simmer for 2½–3 hours until the meat tests done. Remove the meat and take off the rind. Strain the liquid and boil until reduced by half. Pour into a basin and cool, then refrigerate overnight. When set, remove the fat and serve the resulting jelly with the cold pork. Accompany with hot boiled potatoes or a potato salad and curly endive salad. Sprinkle the meat and the jelly with freshly chopped parsley.

This dish is best cold but may be eaten hot. Again reduce the sauce and remove the fat with kitchen paper.

Stuffat tal-majjal, bl'għaġin
Braised pork with pasta

400 g loin or leg of pork
1 onion finely chopped
1 tbsp olive oil
2 cloves garlic
Salt and pepper
Fresh herbs such as thyme, sage or marjoram
2–3 tbsp tomato purée
200 ml stock or water
300 g spaghetti or other pasta

◆ Heat the oil in a heavy saucepan and fry the onion until golden. Add the garlic, seasoning herbs and tomato paste. (If you have to use dried herbs, use them sparingly.) Stir for a minute, then add the pork in one piece and cook gently until it browns on all sides. Add the water or stock, cover and simmer for about 1 hour until the meat is tender. Boil the pasta separately and then either serve it to accompany the meat or make two meals out of it by serving the pasta with the sauce and the meat with potatoes and your choice of vegetables. Maltese families would choose the last option but one could serve the two dishes on different days.

Pulpetti tal-majjal in-bjank

Fricassée of meat balls

800 g minced lean pork
100 g cooked ham, chopped
1 thick slice of white bread
1 tbsp chopped parsley
Pepper
1 egg, beaten
Butter
250 ml stock or water
100–200 g brains, blanched and sliced
100–200 g cooked sweetbreads, sliced (optional)
125 g cooked peas
2 egg yolks, beaten

◆ Put the mince and the ham in a bowl. Soak the slice of bread in milk, squeeze it out and add it to the meat. Add the parsley and season with pepper. Do not add salt at this stage as the ham will be fairly salty. Bind mixture together with the whole beaten egg. Form the mixture into balls, each the size of a walnut and saute gently in butter until brown. Transfer to a deep pan, add the stock, the brains and the sweetbreads, if used. Simmer, uncovered, for 45 minutes. Remove a cupful of the stock and mix it with the beaten egg yolks. Transfer this back to the stock in the pan and stir constantly over very low heat until the sauce thickens to a pouring consistency. Do not let it boil. Some people add slaked corn flour at the same time as the egg yolks to guard against inadvertent curdling.

Pulpettun fil-forn

Baked meat loaf

400 g minced pork
200 g minced beef
1 brain, blanched and sliced
75 g pig's or chicken liver, chopped
1 cup fresh bread crumbs
1 tbsp chopped parsley
1 tbsp grated Parmesan, pecorino or other hard cheese
2 hard-boiled eggs, halved
4 eggs
Salt and pepper
A large piece of caul

◆ Place all the ingredients, except for the raw and hard-boiled eggs and the caul, in a large bowl. Mix thoroughly and season with salt and pepper. Beat the raw eggs and mix them in.

Wash the caul in salted water, rinse it and spread it out to dry in a colander. Open it out wide on the table or working surface and place half the meat mixture on it in an oblong shape. Place the halved hard-boiled eggs on the mixture, evenly spread out, and cover with the rest of the meat mixture. Wrap the loaf in the caul, covering it completely. If caul is unobtainable wrap the loaf instead in greased greaseproof paper.

This is traditionally cooked over potatoes. Peel them and slice them in half horizontally. Lay them out in the roasting tin, pour on some olive oil and water in the same fashion as in the roast beef recipe on page 91, and start them in the oven at 200°C/400°F/gas 6. After 30 minutes, place a rack over the top and lay the meat loaf on this. After 15 minutes reduce the heat to 190°C/375°F/gas 5 and cook for a further 45 minutes

Pulpettun mgħolli

Boiled meat loaf

400 g finely minced pork
400 g finely minced beef
1 or 2 rashers bacon, chopped
1 cup fresh bread crumbs
Salt and pepper
2 tbsp Parmesan or pecorino
2 tbsp chopped parsley
1 onion, grated
4 eggs, beaten
2–3 hard-boiled eggs
Chopped vegetables as in beef broth recipe (page 32)
Chopped parsley to garnish
A piece of muslin and tape to tie it or a large piece of doubled greaseproof paper, oiled

◆ Take the minced meat and add to it the finely chopped bacon and the bread crumbs. Season and add the grated Parmesan, parsley and onion. Bind together with the beaten eggs. Lay out a piece of muslin and spread half the meat mixture on it. Arrange the halved hard-boiled eggs across and cover with the rest of the meat, fold the muslin and tie with tape, like a parcel. You can use a large piece of doubled greasproof paper instead of muslin if you prefer.

Have a large saucepan of boiling water ready, and add the chopped vegetables as for beef broth. Immerse the loaf and simmer gently until firm – about one hour. Remove from the soup and unwrap. Place the loaf on an oval dish, surrounded by the chopped vegetables and sprinkled with fresh chopped parsley.

To make an appetizing soup, reduce the soup to a suitable strength by boiling. Season if required and thicken with semolina, rice or pasta. The meat loaf may also be served cold.

Fenek moqli

Fried rabbit

2 tsp tomato purée
1 rabbit, cut into small joints
1–2 tbsp olive oil
Salt and pepper

◆ Simmer the tomato purée and 100 ml water in a deep pan. Fry the garlic in the oil, but do not let it brown. Transfer the cloves to the tomato mixture. Brown the rabbit joints in the garlic oil. Transfer to the tomato pan. Cover and simmer for about 45 minutes, until the rabbit is tender. Add salt and pepper to taste. Serve with boiled potatoes or chips.

An alternative version is to omit the tomato puree and water and pour a glass or two of red wine over the fried rabbit. Transfer to an earthenware casserole and cook in a slow oven for approximately 1 hour.

Torta tal-fenek
Rabbit pie

1 jointed rabbit
100 g lean pork, cubed
100 g fresh peas, shelled weight
1 onion, sliced
2 tbsp olive oil
2 large ripe tomatoes, peeled and chopped, or 2 tsp tomato purée
100 ml stock and wine, mixeed
Shortcrust or puff pastry (made with 200 g flour)
2 large potatoes, sliced thin
Salt and pepper
Pinch of mixed spice

◆ Dust the rabbit joints with seasoned flour and brown them with the pork in shallow oil. Cool and reserve. Boil the peas, drain and reserve. Fry the onion in 2 tbsp olive oil until softened, add the tomatoes or purée and sufficient stock and wine to make a thick gravy. Cool and reserve.

Roll out the pastry and use half to line a shallow, greased pie dish. Place a layer of the sliced potatoes on the pastry, add the pieces of rabbit, the cooked peas and the gravy. Season with salt, pepper and spice. Moisten the edges of the pastry and cover with a pastry lid, sealing the edges. Glaze with beaten egg. Bake at 220°C/425°F/gas 7 for about 10 minutes. Reduce to 180°C/350°F/gas 4 for 30–45 minutes. Serve hot.

Fenek biz-zalza

Rabbit stew

1 rabbit, jointed, including liver and heart
1–2 tbsp olive oil
2 onions, sliced
2 carrots, sliced
4 cloves of garlic, crushed
200 ml red wine
Salt and pepper
100 g cooked fresh peas

◆ Dust the rabbit joints in seasoned flour. Fry a few at a time in the hot olive oil until they are golden brown. Reserve. In the same pan, fry the onions, carrots and garlic until light brown. Return the rabbit to the pan, add the wine and seasoning. Simmer, covered, until the rabbit is tender, approximately I hour. Add the liver, heart and peas for the last 15 minutes.

The customary way of serving rabbit in Malta is to serve the sauce with spaghetti as a first course, then to have the rabbit, with remaining sauce and chips, as a second course. We would suggest having dishes on successive days.

Fenek bit-tewm u bl-nbid

Garlic-flavoured rabbit

1 rabbit, in joints
375 ml red wine
40 cloves of garlic, peeled
1–2 tbsp olive oil
2–3 bay leaves
Salt and pepper

◆ Pour the wine over the rabbit and leave overnight. Sweat the cloves of garlic in oil in a large frying pan. Do not brown, take out and reserve.

Brown the rabbit on all sides. Transfer to a large casserole and add the wine used as marinade, bay leaves, garlic and seasoning. Cover and cook gently until the rabbit is tender, approximately 1 hour. Add a little more wine if it dries out. Serve hot with potatoes or pasta and green vegetables.

Fenek bil-curry
Curried rabbit

2 tbsp olive or sunflower oil
1 large onion
1 rabbit, jointed
6 cloves of garlic, crushed
1 tbsp curry powder (or vary to taste)
3 carrots, sliced
3 tbsp shelled peas
8 button onions
1 large apple, chopped
200 ml stock or water
Salt

◆ The addition of curry powder to this and one or two other Maltese dishes suggests the British colonial influence. The onions, carrots and peas (typically Maltese) with Anglo-Indian curry and apple is rather an odd mixture.

Fry the onion until golden in the oil, add the rabbit and fry gently until browned. Add the garlic and cook a few minutes longer. Add the curry powder and let it blend in with the onions and garlic. Add the carrots, peas, whole button onions and stock. Simmer, covered, until rabbit and vegetables are cooked, approximately I hour. Add the chopped apple for the last 15 minutes of cooking. Serve hot with boiled or steamed rice.

Tiġieġa-bil-ħaxxu
Stuffing for a chicken (1)

8–10 tbsp bread crumbs
100 g ham, finely chopped
1 tbsp chopped parsley
Salt and pepper
1–2 eggs, beaten
1 hard-boiled egg, chopped
Half a lemon

◆ This stuffing is designed for a boiling fowl such as is used in the recipe for chicken soup on page 34. Proceed as in that recipe, but before setting the fowl to cook, stuff it as follows.

Use a French stick or similar bread to make soft bread crumbs. Mix together the stuffing ingredients. Raw beaten eggs bind the stuffing, enabling you to slice it when cooked. You can omit the beaten eggs and achieve a very good, but crumbly stuffing which will not slice. Rub the outside of the bird with a halved lemon and leave this inside the cavity. Stuff the chicken and sew up the cavity or seal it with a large crust of bread. You can also stuff the chicken between the skin and the flesh of the breast.

Tiġieġa-bil-ħaxxu
Stuffing for a chicken (2)

300 g minced pork
2 tbsp fresh bread crumbs
The chicken liver
1 raw egg, beaten
1 hard-boiled egg, chopped
2 tsp grated onion
2 tsp chopped parsley
50 g chopped ham or bacon

◆ Proceed as above. This stuffing is suitable for roasting or boiling chicken.

Dundjan mimli
Stuffing for turkey

800 g–1 kg minced pork
200 g fresh bread crumbs
100 g finely chopped ham
3 hard-boiled eggs
4–5 eggs, beaten
4 tbsp Parmesan cheese
25–50 g shelled pistachio nuts, coarsely chopped
2 tbsp grated onion
3 tbsp chopped parsley
Salt and pepper

◆ It is customary to stuff the turkey between the skin and flesh of the breast, as well as in the main cavity. This keeps the flesh moist and well flavoured.

Mix all the stuffing ingredients together In a large bowl, adding the hard-boiled eggs at the end. With very clean hands gently separate the skin and flesh at the neck end – you will find this quite easy to do and the skin should not tear if you are careful.

Follow a standard recipe book for roasting the turkey, ensuring that you note the cooking times for a stuffed bird, which always takes longer.

Summien biz-zalza

Braised quail

Quantities are per person

2 quail
1 onion, sliced
1 rasher bacon
150 ml red wine
1 clove garlic
1 bay leaf
Salt and pepper
1 slice toast
1 slice fried bread

◆ Quail were once hunted in Malta as migrants on their way from North Africa to Europe. They can now be purchased as farmed birds from butchers and supermarkets.

If the birds come with their heads, remove the beaks with a sharp knife. Brown the birds in olive oil. Reserve. Fry the onion and garlic in the same oil. Add the bacon and fry some more. Add the wine and boil to reduce for 3 minutes. Add the birds and bay leaf and simmer, covered, for approximately 30 minutes. Taste for seasoning.

Remove the heads and crush them in a mortar with a piece of dry toast. Add a little gravy to keep it moist. Sieve this mixture back into the stewpan. Taste for seasoning and reduce by boiling if the gravy is too thin.

Serve the birds on a piece of fried bread.

Gamiem

Braised pigeon or turtle dove

Pigeon (allow 1 per person)
4 onions, chopped
2 carrots, chopped
1 stick celery, chopped
1 kohl rabi or turnip, peeled and chopped
2 potatoes, peeled and chopped
2 tbsp olive oil
100 g cooked peas
200 g belly pork, diced
300 ml red wine
Salt and pepper

◆ Like the feudal lords of medieval Europe, as rulers of Malta, the Knights of Malta considered pigeons fair game for themselves, but not for the peasantry. Even as late as 1779, the hunting of pigeon, partridge or hare was punishable by 3 years in the galleys. If wood pigeons are used for this dish, close attention should be paid to their tenderness.

Put the birds in a saucepan with half of the chopped onions and the remainder of the vegetables, except the peas. Cover with cold water and simmer, covered, for approximately 2 hours, until the birds are tender. Reserve.

Brown the remainder of the onions in olive oil, add the belly pork and fry for a while longer. Add the red wine and the birds and simmer for 30 minutes. Add the peas, check the seasoning and serve hot.

Pastizz tal-bċieċen

Pigeon pie

6 pigeons
2 onions, sliced
150 ml red wine
3 large potatoes, sliced
Shortcrust or puff pastry (made with 225 g flour)
Salt and pepper
1 egg, beaten, for glaze

◆ Halve or quarter the birds. Fry the onions in olive oil until soft. Add the birds and the wine and simmer, covered, until they are tender. Reserve the pigeons and reduce the gravy by about half by simmering. Fry the sliced potatoes in deep oil until browned.

Line a greased pie dish with half the pastry, add the potatoes, then the birds, then the gravy. Season as you go. Cover with a pastry lid, glaze with beaten egg, and bake at 220°C/425°F/gas 7 for 30–45 minutes.

Borka biz-zalza pikkanti

Wild duck with piquant sauce

1 wild duck, jointed
2 onions or 8–10 pickling onions
2 tsp tomato purée
300 ml red wine
8 black olives, stoned
1 tbsp capers
1 tsp sugar
Salt and pepper

◆ Brown the duck in olive oil. Reserve. Soften the onions in the same oil. Add the tomato puree and a little more than half the wine. Return the duck to the pan. Simmer, covered until the duck is cooked, approximately 45 minutes to 1 hour. Add the remaining wine if the dish shows signs of drying out. Add the olives, capers and sugar about 10 minutes before serving. Check the seasoning.

Gallina jew pluviera biz-zalza

Casseroled woodcock, or plover

2 dressed plovers or woodcock
4 small onions
1 tbsp olive oil
50 g butter
1 bay leaf
300 ml white wine
Salt and pepper

◆ Plovers are no longer acceptable as a table bird, but woodcock are available from game dealers in Britain at the right season.

Halve the onions and put them with the birds in a pan with the oil and butter. Fry gendy until lightly browned. Add the bay leaf and white wine. Simmer, covered, until the birds are cooked, approximately I hour. Check the seasoning and serve hot.

Ħaruf fil-forn

Roast lamb

1 leg of lamb
1-n2 cloves garlic, slivered
Salt and pepper
6 large potatoes, thickly sliced lengthwise
2 large onions, sliced
2 tbsp olive oil
2 tbsp fresh bread crumbs
1 sprig of fresh rosemary
Fresh parsley, chopped

◆ Remove as much fat as possible from the lamb, using a sharp knife. Score the flesh. Make incisions in the meat and insert slivers of garlic. Season the joint. Place a layer of potatoes and onions in a greased baking tin. Pour the oil over the potatoes and onions. Rub oil and seasoning on the lamb, then sprinkle with the bread crumbs and spikes of rosemary. Cook at 220°C/425°F/gas 7 for 30 minutes, then reduce to 180°C/350°F/gas 4. Allow 25 minutes per 400 g plus 25 minutes resting time. Turn the potatoes and onions over once during cooking. Finish with plenty of chopped parsley before serving.

Frikassija tal-ħaruf

Lamb fricassée

2 onions, thinly sliced
15 g butter
800 g lamb cutlets or diced lamb, suitable for stewing
2 tbsp olive oil
15 g butter
200 g shelled peas
Strip of lemon peel, without pith
Salt and pepper
Juice of half a lemon
2 egg yolks
Grated lemon rind
Fresh parsley, chopped

◆ Put the onions in a saucepan with 2 tsp of water and cook over a low heat, stirring constantly, until the moisture evaporates. See that the onion remains white. Add the butter to the pan and cook until the onion is soft, taking care not to let it brown. Fry the pieces of lamb in more oil and butter in a separate pan until they are golden brown. Add to the onion mixture, add 20 ml cold water, the peas and the strip of lemon rind. Cover and simmer gently until the meat is tender. Check the seasoning. Take off the heat. Beat the egg yolks in a small bowl with a little of the gravy. Add to the lamb. Return to a very low heat and stir until the sauce thickens. Do not boil.

Lastly add the lemon juice and a little more grated lemon rind. Sprinkle with chopped parsley. Serve hot with boiled rice or mashed potatoes. Kid can be cooked in the same way

Fritturi tal-moħħ

Brain fritters

2 brains
2 eggs
2 tbsp finely chopped parsley
Salt and pepper

◆ There are problems attendant on buying brains in Britain as a result of BSE. You may have more confidence in the offal available in other countries. If you buy frozen brains you will find them extremely difficult to skin, so buy fresh if you possibly can.

Soak the brains in cold, salted water and peel off the membranes. Blanch in boiling, salted and vinegared water for 10 minutes. Drain and cool. Cut into neat slices.

Separate the eggs, beat the whites until stiff then blend in the yolks. Add the chopped parsley and seasoning. Dip the slices of brain into the beaten egg and fry at once in hot olive oil until golden. Serve with wedges of lemon and fried potatoes.

Torta tal-kirxa
Tripe pie

800 g tripe
1 large aubergine
2 onions, sliced
3 tbsp tomato purée
1 bay leaf
Shortcrust pastry (made with 200 g flour)
1 egg, beaten, for glaze

◆ Wash the tripe thoroughly, rinsing it several times. If not already blanched, boil until just tender, drain, cool and cut it into small pieces or mince it.

Not all tripe pies are made with aubergine as suggested here. Slice the vegetable thinly, mix with salt and leave to drain in a colander for I hour. Fry the slices in olive oil until brown, drain on kitchen paper, cool, and reserve.

Fry the onion in olive oil until soft, add the tomato purée diluted with 250 ml water. Simmer for half an hour, adding the bay leaf. Stir in the tripe. Allow to cool.

Roll out slightly more than half the pastry and line a shallow, greased pie dish. Put in the tripe and the aubergine. Cover with the remaining pastry, seal the edges well and glaze. Cook at 200°C/400°F/gas 6 for 15 minutes, then at 180°C/350°F/gas 4 for 30 minutes.

Kirxa fil-forn
Baked tripe

1.25 kg tripe
2 onions, sliced
425 g tin peeled tomatoes
2 aubergines
6 eggs
50 g cooked ham, chopped
Salt and pepper
3 tbsp grated Parmesan
Soft bread crumbs
Butter

◆ Prepare the tripe as in the previous recipe. Cut into small pieces. Fry the sliced onions in olive oil. Add the tripe and the tomatoes, mixing them in. Simmer for 30 minutes. Allow to cool. Beat the eggs and add them to the tripe mixture with the chopped ham and 2 tbsp cheese. Check seasoning and reserve. Prepare and cook the aubergines as before. Reserve.

Butter an oven-proof dish, make alternate layers of aubergine and tripe, starting with the vegetable. Top with 1 tbsp cheese, some soft bread crumbs and a few knobs of butter. Cook at 400°C/200°F/gas 6 for 40–50 minutes until the eggs are set. Serve very hot.

Kirxa moqlija
Fried tripe

400 g tripe
2 eggs
1 tbsp finely chopped parsley
1 cup of fine bread or galletti *crumbs*
Salt and pepper

◆ Prepare the tripe as before and allow to get cold. Cut into squares and dip them in beaten egg and parsley, seasoned with salt and pepper. Then coat with the bread or galletti crumbs. Fry in olive oil and butter until brown, drain on kitchen paper. Serve with wedges of lemon, crusty bread or chipped potatoes and follow with a salad.

Fwied moqli bir-rand u l-ħall
Fried liver with bay leaves and vinegar

8 large cubes of pigs' liver
A piece of caul
Bay leaves
Salt and pepper
2 cloves garlic, crushed
1 tbsp wine vinegar

◆ Wrap each piece of liver together with bay leaf, seasoning and garlic in a portion of caul. Fry in olive oil making sure that the liver does not get overcooked or hard. Remove to a hot dish and reserve. De-glaze the pan with the vinegar, then pour over the liver parcels. Serve hot, with mashed potatoes.

Some cooks use stock or water to de-glaze, rather than vinegar.

Fwied fis-seffud
Liver kebabs

400 g pigs' liver
Piece of caul (optional)
200 g bacon, diced
Bay leaves
6–8 slices of white bread, spread with olive oil and cut into squares

◆ Cut the liver into squares and wrap each in a piece of caul if available. Take fine skewers and thread them with liver, bacon, a bay leaf and a square of bread alternately until all the ingredients have been used. Grill under a moderate heat for about 10 minutes until the liver is cooked but not overdone. Serve with lemon wedges, salad, fried potatoes or crusty bread.

Zalzett ta'Malta

Maltese sausages

1.75 kg pork, coarsely minced – a mixture of fat and lean
90 g sea salt
45 g crushed black peppercorns
45 g crushed coriander seeds
5 cloves of garlic, crushed
4 tbsp chopped parsley
Pork intestines (the butcher will supply)

◆ Most butchers in Malta sell these sausages, but you can make them yourself.

Mix the pork with all the other ingredients, except the intestines. Wash the intestines thoroughly in several changes of cold salted water. Using a funnel or sausage-making attachment, fill the skins with the mixture, then tie with string at 50–75 mm intervals. Prick each sausage with a fork and hang in the coolest place possible for 2–3 days. The butcher who gave us this recipe said that on a day when a strong north wind is blowing they can be ready to eat in 24 hours. In the winter it is thought safe to eat them raw after sufficient hanging. Alternatively, the sausages may be simmered for 15 minutes in water to which a halved onion, peppercorns and bay leaves have been added. They may be eaten boiled, grilled or fried, or cooked according to the recipe for pork 'en daube' (page 100).

To save the trouble of making sausages, mix the ingredients (but use much less salt) with 2 beaten eggs. Roll into balls the size of a large walnut, or into sausage shapes, and grill or fry until thoroughly cooked.

❖❖❖❖❖

We add here one example of a meat dish immensely suited to foods we grow in Malta which in different circumstances, might have become part of our repertoire. From the Al Baghdadi Cookery Book, Rummanija takes its name from our rummien (pomegranates). The recipe is dated 1226. It appears in the chapter entitled "Sour Dishes". The recipes in this book are of Persian origin and were discovered by Dr Daoud Celebi in 1934 and translated by Professor A. J. Arberry. The author was Muhammad ibn Hasan ibn Muhammad ibn al-Karim al-Katib al-Baghdadi.

Rummanija

◆ Cut fat meat into middling pieces and put into the saucepan with a little scented salt and cover with water. Boil and remove the scum thoroughly. Strip egg plant of its black skin and split it well; peel and split onions also. Peel a gourd, remove the pith and seeds and cut into strips. Throw all these into the saucepan after half-boiling them in a separate pot. Add coriander, cumin, cinnamon, pepper, mastic and some sprigs of mint and cook well. Now take sour pomegranates, squeeze very well in the hand, strain and throw into the saucepan. Rub in dry mint. Pound a little garlic and leave this also in the pot. A chicken, quartered, may be placed in the saucepan to cook with the meat. Leave over a slow fire for an hour, then remove.

This dish seems easily adaptable to a 21st century kitchen. Our only guidance would be to simmer at every stage and not to boil. The meat could be beef or lamb or pork (for non-Muslims).

The scented salt "milh Mutajjab" referred to is complicated. "Take large pieces of rock Andarani salt, put into a new earthenware jar and close the mouth; leave in a hot oven for a whole day, then bring out. When cold, mill fine. Take coriander, sesame, shuniz, hemp, poppy, cumin, fennel and leaves of asafoetida and aniseed. Toast all and mix in. After milling the salt, colour it by placing for a day and night in water in which saffron had been dissolved, then dry and mill again. It may also be coloured with sumach juice or vermillion. If desired it may be dyed green with beet juice."

We do not suggest that you embark on making this salt but you might like to try some of the spices mentioned to your dish of Rummanija and you will be preparing a dish first devised almost 800 years ago!

VEĠETARJANIŻMU U ID-DIETA MALTIJA

VEGETARIANISM AND THE MALTESE DIET

A few notes on vegetarianism for non-vegetarians

'Pelagia looked down on her cargo of mucilaginous animals and poked them with her finger when they tried to crawl out of the pot. She began to feel very sorry for them . . . Prodding at the snails she was saddened by the cruelty of a world in which the living can only live by predation on creatures weaker than themselves. It seemed a poor way to order a universe.'

From de Bernières, Louis 1994 'Captain Corelli's Mandolin' London. Minerva Press

'Malta ħanina-ħobż u sardina'
Old Tunisian saying

All the evidence points to meat eating as a rare luxury for the majority of Maltese and Gozitan people, until relatively recently. As Carmeo Cassar tells us (page 3) 'common people (sic) dreamt of consuming meat, essentially because their diet consisted primarily of vegetables' – someone must have been eating meat, however, or there wouldn't have had anything to dream about. He quotes Mgr. Visconti writing in 1582 that 'the greater part of the people eat 'pane misturato' (dark coarse bread made of wheat and barley), vegetables and latticini (ġbejniet?)'. In 'The Last of the Crusaders' de Cavaliero refers to a Baron Riedesel who noted in 1773 that the Maltese 'still lived frugally on bread, peppers, onions and anchovies; (ħobż biż-żejt in fact). In 1804 de Boisgelin recorded that the usual diet consisted of 'a clove of garlic, or an onion, anchovies dipped in oil and salted fish'. As in every other part of the world, we imagine, the poor and the wealthy ate very different foods and still do.

While this is most definitely not a vegetarian cookery book (and the authors are not vegetarians) we want to emphasise the importance of vegetables in our cuisine and to make a few comments on vegetarianism which is increasing in our islands, such that we now have a Vegetarian Society (Għaqda Veġetarjana ta' Malta). There are now a number of vegetarian restaurants, of which one, at least, is outstandingly good by any standard.

In contemplating a vegetarian diet what are the chief considerations? Are human beings omnivores, herbivores or carnivores? There are many academic works to support every side of the argument but what can be said with certainty is that human beings can most certainly survive and be perfectly healthy without eating animals or animal products. Primitive societies teach us that the regular pattern of their diets (in different ecological environments) was, before Western intervention, in tune with that environment – thus Eskimos (the Inuit) relied heavily on fish and seals while sub-Saharan African hunter/gatherers did not eat meat frequently but obtained their protein chiefly from nuts and legumes. Meat was nearly always relished and very much enjoyed when it was obtained; the fat is particularly prized in some societies – presumably because of its rarity value. There are many examples of meat forming the centre of grand religious and social celebrations, from all over the world, but over the centuries primitive societies have not disturbed the ecological balance of their habitats and regard culling as a Western interference.

Vegetarianism, of course, has for centuries been at the core of the Hindu, Jain, Buddhist and other religions though some Hindu castes do eat meat other than cows. Other religions (with the exception of Christianity, which prohibits no meat at all) forbid only one kind of meat (e.g. pork) and the source of such prohibitions will almost certainly have had some practical or health connotations when they first originated. In Western cultures the movement (for want of a better word) is on the increase and some would argue that it is only the affluent who can afford to indulge in it, since people on very low incomes consume little animal protein anyway. People who become vegetarians may be broadly divided into two groups, though there are some links between them. First there are those which relate to individual interests (even selfish ones) – such as the cost of meat and fish and the danger to health; secondly those which relate to socio/political/environmental and religious concerns. The reasons of cost are obvious and need no further explanation but it is usually those who have enjoyed meat and fish eating in the past and who are now less well off, rather than those who have always been poor, who make the decision. Health issues concern the over-consumption of animal protein in general and red meat in particular, too much of which is believed to contribute to heart disease, cancer, arthritis and other conditions. There is considerable anxiety also about the use of hormones as growth promoters in animals raised commercially for food. People who stop eating red meat on cost and/or health grounds are, therefore, unlikely to become vegetarians in the true sense of the word, but merely reduce their consumption to a greater or less extent. They could be described as non-meat eaters.

Awareness of what vegetarianism is about is scant in many parts of the world, including Malta and one meets some strange social responses to guests who announce to their party hosts that they are vegetarians. Why, for example, do buffet parties often include a dish of prawns especially prepared for vegetarian guests who, of course, shudder at the thought of eating such helpless little creatures. Other hosts are positively hostile and accuse the vegetarians of bad manners and causing them inconvenience. One solution is to prepare an entirely vegetarian meal and a dish or two of meat for the meat eaters – that would make a change!

Turning to wider social and ecological reasons – there are two. Supporters of the first argue that human enjoyment of food should not be based on killing or interfering with the freedom of animals, or using them to make profits. The second is that a fair distribution of protein to the people of the entire earth can only be achieved if the consumption of animal protein is heavily reduced. This is because sources of protein produced as grain, pulses, cereals and nuts, if consumed directly in this form, feed approximately 80% more people than if the same area of land is used for animals to graze, which in turn are eaten by people. Moore Lappé (pp. 5–9) puts it like this: 'a cow must be fed 21 pounds of protein in order to produce 1 pound of protein for human consumption' – admittedly other animals are more efficient; a pig requires a mere 8.3 lbs and a chicken 5.5 lbs. An acre of cereal produces 5 times more protein than an acre devoted to meat production.

Consider, also for example, roasted peanuts and their place in the rich economies. While it is true that they are a major source of protein for the growing number of vegetarians in the West, they are also consumed in vast quantities, as a snack, by people who also consume the main source of their protein as meat and fish. Yet those same nuts (a troublesome extra for most of us) could be a rich source of inexpensive protein for non-meat eaters all over the world – particularly for those who live in the regions where the peanuts are actually grown! What has taken place in some parts of our globe is a disruption of the traditional food production system by the combined effect of drought, and a number of adverse human interventions such as war, cash-cropping, colonialism (and its modern day residues) and a world trade system which is skewed in the interests of Western economies.

Serious committed vegetarians, themselves, fall into two groups – lacto vegetarians who consume animal products, such as milk and eggs, but never the animals themselves, and vegans who go further, arguing that not only should humans not derive enjoyment from eating animals who have been deliberately killed, but also that they should not be used as vehicles for our food, since this interferes with their freedom and forces an unnatural way of life on them which, in itself, is cruel. There are two examples of such cruelty – battery chickens and veal calves, both of whom suffer immense pain and suffering in order that we humans may eat veal and more eggs than are good for us. The great Mahatma Gandhi, who devoted his life to his fellow humans, carried the vegan position to extremes and did so for all the reasons described. Adolf Hitler was also a vegetarian because he loved animals.

Finally, the ecological, scientific and religious philosophies are beginning to come closer together. Christian interpretations of the Book of Genesis (in some circles) are being re-examined and re-interpreted to mean that all creatures, including humans, are in a symbiotic relationship with the earth and with one another without the domination of humans. David Steindl-Rast (in Capra F. et al 'Belonging to the Universe' pp. 91–94) puts it like this, referring to Genesis:

'then comes the part when we are put into the Garden (of Eden) "to tend it and keep it." That is where the sense of (human) responsibility comes in. Stewardship, rather than exploitative domination is the crux of that passage. Unfortunately the Book of Genesis has been misinterpreted and misused to justify a lot of destructive things.' Tending and keeping the garden is our responsibility – for as human beings we need not destroy nature though we are the only creatures that have the frightful power to do so.

Yet, we also find in Genesis (ix. 3) 'Every moving thing that liveth shall be meat for you;'.

By the middle of the next century this may well become a purely academic argument since the rate at which genetic modification is progressing (if that is the right word) is so breathtakingly fast and frightening. Scientists can already govern the functions of plants so successfully that, in the words of the geneticist Steve Jones (partly tongue in cheek) 'plants will soon do almost everything and . . . animals will fade in importance as – perhaps – the salmon flavoured banana takes over'. It is unlikely that anyone reading this will ever have to eat a salmon-flavoured banana, but we should not underestimate the seriousness of the message. The debate continues.

HCG

GĦAĠIN U ROSS
PASTA AND RICE

Pasta and bread are the staple foods of the Maltese and Gozitan people. Until perhaps 30 years ago, spaghetti and macaroni were the commonest shapes, but of late, lasagne and cannelloni have found their way into most of our kitchens. We have not included any recipes for these, since we regard them as purely Italian. For the same reason, we do not include a recipe for pizza, although now firmly established as a favourite food. Maltese cooks frequently add *rikotta* to lasagne recipes, which does not appear in the Italian version.

When we were growing up, spaghetti with tomato sauce was a mainstay of Maltese diet. Most families would eat it twice a week. In summer one would use fresh tomatoes, abundant and cheap, but at other times tinned or purée. It was once a common sight to see housewives in small, simple grocers' shops buying a meagre *nofs qwart* (100 g) of purée, wrapped in a small square of greaseproof paper, sufficient for that day's lunch. Fortunately, those poverty-stricken days are over.

Sunday is the day for *timpana* or *ross fil-forn*, although the first is more popular. During the British occupation, it was not unusual for timpana to be followed by a joint of meat, but this is mercifully less common now. A well-made timpana makes a meal a feast. Baked in the lightest puff pastry, rich with sauce, meat, eggs and Parmesan, it is like a three-course meal rolled into one. If you love *timpana*, make up for it by eating nothing else until the next day.

Timpana
Macaroni in a pastry case

2 tbsp olive oil
1 large onion, sliced
50 g unsmoked bacon, finely chopped
2 cloves garlic, crushed
400 g minced beef and pork
Salt and pepper
3 tbsp tomato purée
400 g tin of peeled tomatoes
125 ml beef or chicken stock
1 bay leaf
Grated fresh nutmeg
1 calf brain (optional)
200 g chicken livers
400 g macaroni
4 large eggs, beaten
4 heaped tbsp grated Parmesan
Puff, flaky or shortcrust pastry (made with 200 g flour)
Beaten egg for glazing

◆ This is a dish for special occasions, although you might not think so when you observe the frequency with which it is eaten all over our islands. In the days when people ate too much, it used to be served as a starter, but for most people today *timpana* stands on its own. In his novel *Il Gattopardo*, Giuseppe di Lampedusa refers to a similar dish. *Timpana* is almost certainly Sicilian in origin.

To make the sauce, heat the oil and fry the onions gently until golden, add bacon, garlic and minced meat, salt and pepper. Use little salt at this stage. Stir well and cook for 15 minutes. Add the tomato purée, the tomatoes, stock and the bay leaf. Grate in some nutmeg. Simmer, covered, for about 30 minutes, then uncovered for another 30 minutes.

If you live in a country where brain is still available, soak for 1 hour in cold, salted and vinegared water, then remove as much as you can of the membranes. Blanch in boiling water, with 1 tsp vinegar, for about 10 minutes. Cool. Slice fairly thickly. If using chicken livers, remove any discoloured parts, chop into large pieces and fry lightly in butter. Cool and remove the stringy bits.

Boil the macaroni in plenty of salted water until *al dente*. Pour a cup of cold water into the pan as soon as the pasta is cooked. It is important it remains underdone so that it will retain its shape and texture at the end. Drain. Mix the meat and tomato into the macaroni, add the eggs, the cheese and season again, if required, with salt and pepper. Mix all well together in a large bowl. Leave to cool.

Roll out approximately ¾ of the pastry to fit a large oven-proof dish. Some cooks like to use a large loose-bottomed cake tin. Put in a layer of macaroni and meat, then a layer of chicken livers and the sliced brain and cover with the remaining macaroni. Cover with pastry, moistening the edges that come together. Glaze with egg. Bake at 220°C/425°F/gas 7 for 15 minutes. Reduce to 180°C/350°F/gas 4 and continue cooking for 30 minutes.

When aubergines are in season you can add some slices, previously poached or fried in olive oil, instead of the livers and brain.

The ideal *timpana* slices neatly. This is achieved by careful cooking of the macaroni in the initial stages. You will find that it slices better if allowed to stand for about 30 minutes after it comes out of the oven.

Mqarrun fil-forn
Baked macaroni

◆ This is made the same way as *timpana*, but without the pastry. The brain and livers can also be omitted. Instead, it is customary to sprinkle semolina or fine bread crumbs over the base and sides of the greased tin or oven-proof dish in which the macaroni is cooked. A perfectly baked *mqarrun* is crunchy on the outside and moist inside. Both this dish and *timpana* improve with keeping. Reheat any leftovers thoroughly in a moderate oven for about half an hour.

When they are in season, you may add slices of fried aubergine, or use a Greek variation and pour over a rich béchamel sauce enriched with beaten eggs before you put it in the oven.

Mqarrun maħmuġ
'Dirty' macaroni

◆ Use the ingredients (except the pastry) deployed for *timpana* and *mqarrun fil forn*, except this time, omit the eggs. Cook the macaroni and sauce separately. Turn them both into a large saucepan and heat very well, stirring frequently. Pieces of fried aubergine may be added. Serve hot, accompanied with plenty of Parmesan. Before serving, garnish with lots of chopped parsley.

Forma tal-mqarrun
Macaroni mould

2 large aubergines
1 onion, finely chopped
1 tbsp olive oil
2 cloves garlic, crushed
300 g minced beef and pork
4 tsp tomato purée
125 ml beef or chicken stock
1 bay leaf
300 g macaroni
2 eggs, beateb
2 tbsp grated Parmesan
Salt and pepper

◆ Peel and slice the aubergines, then salt and drain them. Dry on kitchen roll.

Heat the oil and fry the onions gently until golden, add garlic and minced meat, salt and pepper. Stir well and cook for 15 minutes. Add the tomato purée, stock and the bay leaf. Simmer, covered, for about 30 minutes, then uncovered for another 30 minutes.

Boil the macaroni until *al dente*. Drain and cool slightly. Mix with the sauce. Add the beaten eggs and cheese and check seasoning.

Fry the aubergine in additional olive oil until golden. Drain again on kitchen roll.

Grease a pudding basin and arrange the aubergine round the base and sides, leaving no spaces. Chop up any remaining slices and mix with the macaroni. Spoon this into the basin, cover with its lid, greaseproof paper or foil. Steam gently for 1 hour in a large covered saucepan that has water sufficient to come half-way up the basin. Turn out and serve hot, with more Parmesan. A vegetarian version can be made by substituting more aubergines, mushrooms, or courgettes for the meat. You could also add some torn basil leaves.

Għaġin Grieg jew Tork

Greek or Turkish style pasta

750 g minced beef and pork
3 rashers unsmoked bacon
4 large onions, sliced
100 g butter
Chicken stock
Salt and pepper
4 heaped tbsp Parmesan
750 g pasta

◆ Don't describe this dish as Turkish to your Greek friends (nor vice-versa). The best kinds of pasta to use for this dish are *penne* (Italian) or *żibeċ* (Maltese).

Put the meat, bacon, onions and butter in a saucepan. Cover with chicken stock, and add seasoning. Cook on a slow fire for 2 hours. At the end of cooking, add 1 tbsp Parmesan.

Boil the pasta in salted water until just tender. Drain. Combine the pasta and meat sauce (perhaps with more butter) and the rest of the Parmesan. Heat thoroughly, stirring all the while. Serve hot.

Għaġin bl'irkotta

Pasta with ***rikotta***

750 g pasta
600 g rikotta
3–4 eggs, beaten
1 tbsp chopped parsley
Salt and pepper
Butter
Grated fresh Parmesan

◆ Use *rigatoni* (*makkarunelli* in Maltese), *conchiglie* (*bebbux*) or *cappelletti* (*fdewwex*).

Boil the pasta until tender. Mash the *rikotta* with a fork in a bowl and mix in the eggs, chopped parsley and seasoning. Drain the pasta and return to the pan. Add the *rikotta* mixture and stir thoroughly to make sure the pasta is heated through. Try not to overcook the eggs. Add a big knob of butter. This can be served with a plain tomato sauce (page 216) and grated Parmesan.

Some people prefer to omit the eggs as they can dry out the dish. In this case increase the butter. The tomato sauce is also optional.

For another version, use the pasta known in Malta as gnocchi. These are large shells. Fill them (prior to cooking) with the rikotta and beaten egg mixture. Drop carefully into boiling water and simmer (to prevent the filling hardening and falling out). Serve with tomato sauce and Parmesan.

Ravjul
Rikotta-filled ravioli

For the dough
200 g plain flour
Pinch of salt
150 g fine semolina
2 beaten eggs

For the filling
400 g rikotta
2 eggs, beaten
4 tbsp grated Parmesan
Salt and Pepper
1 tbsp finely chopped parsley

◆ To prepare the dough, sieve flour and salt into a bowl and add semolina. Add the eggs and knead until pliable and elastic. If too stiff, add a fraction of cold water. Set aside.

Prepare the filling by mashing the *rikotta* and adding the beaten eggs, cheese, seasoning and parsley.

Roll out portions of the dough as thinly as possible into oblong strips. Place generous teaspoons of filling down or along one side, leaving a small space between each little mound of filling. Fold over the dough and press down at the edge and between every section then cut with a fluted cutter into a half-moon shape. Repeat the process with the remaining dough and filling.

Simmer the ravioli (do not boil) in a large pan for about 10–15 minutes or until the edges test done. A tablespoon of oil added to the water will prevent them sticking. Stir once or twice during cooking.

Drain and serve very hot with a good tomato sauce to which fresh peas have been added. Accompany with freshly grated Parmesan. Some cooks prepare the *ravjul* in advance, place them in layers in an oven-proof dish with tomato sauce and cheese, cover with knobs of butter and heat them through in a moderate oven.

If semolina is not available use flour instead, a total of 350 g would suffice.

We dedicate this recipe to the memory of Duminka Farrugia, an exceptional cook and very loved member of our immediate family in the years after World War II. She made the best *ravjul* we have ever tasted.

Għaġin bl'inċova

Spaghetti with anchovy sauce

100 g anchovy fillets, chopped
3 tbsp olive oil
2 cloves of garlic, crushed
400 g spaghetti

◆ Heat the oil and add the crushed garlic and the anchovy. Boil the pasta until *al dente* and immediately mix in the anchovy mixture. The traditional accompaniment is crushed *galletti* (page 183) and was eaten on Good Friday. However, you can serve grated Parmesan and perhaps some finely chopped parsley too.

Froġa tal-għaġin

Spaghetti 'omelette'

200 g cooked spaghetti
1–2 eggs
Salt and pepper
1 tbsp parsley, chopped
3 tbsp grated Parmesan
2 tbspn olive oil

◆ This is a good way of using left over pasta of any kind. The quantities described here are enough for two people.

If the pasta has become dry, soften it by pouring boiling water over it and draining. Beat the eggs in a large bowl, add the cold pasta, half the Parmesan, seasoning and parsley. Mix. Heat olive oil in a large frying pan. Spread the pasta over the bottom of the pan. Cook until the underneath is set. Turn on to a plate and slip back into the pan on the reverse side. Cook until golden; serve with chopped parsley and the rest of the Parmesan.

Forma tar-ross

Rice mould

300 g long grain rice
4 cups meat sauce
4 tbsp grated Parmesan
3 tbsp cooked peas
3 hard-boiled eggs, chopped
Chopped fresh parsley
Salt and pepper

◆ Boil the rice in plenty of water for just 10–12 minutes. Drain. While still hot mix the rice with enough meat sauce to give it a good colour, save the rest. Use the meat sauce as prepared in the recipe for *timpana* on page 126. Add the cheese, peas, the chopped eggs, and the parsley. Season well. Turn the mixture into a lightly greased pudding basin. Cover. Steam in a covered saucepan for 45 minutes. Turn out and pour over the remaining sauce, heated through, or serve it separately with grated Parmesan. An envelope or two of saffron may be mixed into the sauce, at the beginning, but it is not essential.

Ross fil-forn
Baked rice

2 onions, chopped
2 cloves garlic, crushed
3 rashers unsmoked bacon, chopped
2 tbsp olive oil
50 g butter
100 g minced beef
200 g minced pork
400 g tin tomatoes
Salt and pepper
100 g chicken livers
Pinch grated nutmeg
1–2 tsp saffron
3 cups chicken stock
1½ cups long grain rice
3 eggs, beaten
75 g grated Parmesan cheese
2 brains

◆ This is one of the best loved Maltese dishes, although few restaurants present a really good example of it. The method is in essence that of an English baked rice pudding, but that is where the resemblance ends. Perfection is not easily achieved, even experienced cooks get disappointing results.

Cook the onion, bacon and garlic in a mixture of olive oil and butter until soft. After 5 minutes add the minced beef and pork. Cook until the meat begins to brown. Add the tin of tomatoes. Season. Simmer for 30–40 minutes until you have a thickish mixture.

Blanch the cleaned and chopped chicken livers for just 1 minute in boiling water, drain and add to the sauce. Add some freshly grated nutmeg. Infuse the saffron in a little heated chicken stock for 5 minutes.

Mix the rice, the stock, the saffron infusion (and the threads), and the sauce together. Add the beaten eggs and Parmesan. Transfer to a well greased oven-proof dish.

Soak the brains in salt water for 1 hour, peel off the membranes, then blanch in salted water acidulated with 1 tbsp vinegar for 10 minutes. Cut into large dice and push them into the surface of the rice. If you live in a country where brains are no longer available, or you would rather not enjoy their distinctive texture, they can be omitted from the recipe.

Cook at 180°C/350°F/gas 4 for 60–90 minutes. Test after 1 hour and return to the oven if the rice is not yet cooked or the liquid not all absorbed.

This dish can be easily adapted for vegetarians by substituting fried aubergines, mushrooms, courgettes or artichoke hearts for the meat.

It requires practice to turn out a good *ross fil-forn* so follow the instructions carefully. Our family tends to be liberal with saffron – we use a good two to three teaspoons for every three cups of rice. Use saffron threads, accept no substitutes. It is said that the Phoenicians so loved their saffron, it accompanied them wherever they went. The Knights of Malta also seem to have had a special fondness for saffron. This fact alone is an indicator of the affluent lifestyle they enjoyed while ruling our islands.

Ross bl-irkotta

Baked rice with ***rikotta***

400 g rice
400 g rikotta
3 eggs, beaten
2 tbsp chopped parsley
1 tbsp grated Parmesan
Salt and pepper
Fine bread or galletti *crumbs*

◆ Boil the rice for 10–12 minutes until just tender. Drain and rinse under the hot tap to remove starch. Mix the *rikotta* with the eggs, parsley, Parmesan and seasoning. Stir well with a wooden fork. Butter an oven-proof dish and dust with fine bread or *galletti* crumbs. Spoon in the mixture and dot liberally with butter. Bake at 180°C/350°F/gas 4 for 30 minutes, until hot. Serve hot, either with a tomato sauce (page 216) or just as it is.

Timpana tar-ross bil-qaqoċċ

Timpana of rice with artichokes

For the pastry

200 g plain flour
100 g butter
3 tbsp milk

For the filling

1½ cups long grain rice
1 large onion, finely chopped
1 clove garlic, crushed
2 tbsp olive oil and a little butter
100 g chicken livers, chopped
6–8 fresh artichoke hearts
250 ml chicken stock (or ½ wine, ½ stock)
1 tbsp tomato purée
1 tspn saffron
Salt and pepper
3 tbsp Parmesan, grated
3 eggs, beaten
Melted butter or a little beaten egg

◆ This dish has been cooked in our family since our great-grandmother's days. It figures in the recipe book *Ctieb tal Chcina* mentioned in the bibliography, although grandmother added the artichoke hearts which are incorporated in this modern version.

Prepare the pastry in the usual way and keep cold. Boil the rice for 10–12 minutes. Drain and rinse under cold running water. Reserve. Cook the onions and garlic in oil and butter until soft and turning golden. Add the chicken livers and the artichoke hearts, cut in half. Pour over the stock, mixed with tomato puree and the saffron. Simmer until the artichokes are tender. Mix this sauce into the rice, using a wooden fork so as not to break the grains. Season and taste. Add the Parmesan and the eggs. Cool. Line a greased deep dish or loosebottomed cake tin with two-thirds of the pastry. Spoon in the cold filling and cover with the remainder. Decorate with pastry leaves and brush with butter or beaten egg. Bake at 200°C/400°F/gas 6 for 10–15 minutes, then at 180°C/350°F/gas 4 for 30 minutes. Serve hot with more grated Parmesan.

Sauces for pasta

To conclude this chapter we add some suggestions of our own as accompaniments to pasta. The cookery of Malta no more stands still than does the cookery of any other country: new influences make their mark.

Aubergine

Add chopped aubergines to a tomato sauce, with some fresh or crushed dried red chili pepper. Alternatively, fry very thin rounds of aubergine or courgettes in olive oil, drain on kitchen paper and serve in a separate dish, sprinkled with parsley, to accompany spaghetti with tomato sauce.

Artichoke hearts and courgettes

Mix halved fresh artichoke hearts and *qarabagħli* or courgettes. Cook them, covered, with some crushed garlic and parsley in a mixture of olive oil and butter. Mix into hot pasta and add plenty of grated Paremsan and seasoning.

Courgettes and broad beans

Dice the courgettes or *qarabagħli* small, the same size as the beans. Cook them in the same way as detailed for artichoke hearts, above. Ideally, the inner shell of the beans should be removed.

Cauliflower (or spinach) and garlic

Divide a cauliflower into tiny pieces and parboil for just a few minutes. Drain well and then fry until golden in olive oil, together with some crushed garlic and finely chopped chili. Mix with very hot pasta and add plenty of Parmesan and freshly chopped parsley or basil. Spinach can be used instead of cauliflower, in which case, cook it until tender, drain well and chop it in the colander with the side of a plate. Finish in the same way as above.

Rocket

Soften some chopped and washed rocket leaves in a mixture of olive oil and butter. Add a little crushed garlic. Fry or grill some roughly chopped smoked bacon until crisp and mix well into hot pasta with the rocket. Season generously.

Mushrooms

Cultivated mushrooms are now widely available on the islands. For this recipe you need a generous quantity, say 500 g. Slice them thinly. Cook two finely chopped onions and some garlic in a mixture of olive oil and butter. Add the mushrooms and cook until soft and golden. Sprinkle in a dessertspoonful of plain flour and allow it to absorb the juices. Season well, adding nutmeg if you wish, and possibly finish with extra butter or some double cream.

Tuna and nut sauce

Mix pine nuts, walnuts or broken cashews, some garlic, plenty of parsley and a tin of good quality tuna fish preserved in oil. Use a blender to process this into a puree, or pound (laboriously) in a large pestle and mortar. Mix into the pasta, seasoning generously with black pepper.

ĦAXIX
VEGETABLES

In the Maltese islands, as in other parts of the Mediterranean, vegetables are never regarded as a mere accompaniment to the main course but as dishes in their own right. Like all mediterraneans and middle-eastern people, we go in for stuffing vegetables, baking them and putting them into soup: we fry them stew them and put them into pies. Vegetables make a main course at supper time, served as a warm salad with an oil and lemon juice or vinegar dressing. Stuffed artichokes make a popular and healthy supper dish. When they are ready to eat pour some olive oil and vinegar (or lemon juice) on to your plate, tilt it by placing a knife or fork underneath, at the back of the plate. This dressing will collect into a little pool at the front into which you dip your artichoke leaves. Lettuce, raw or gently cooked and accompanied with a vinaigrette makes a delicious light dish. Cos lettuce abounds and it is the round cabbage lettuce (Ħass kabuċċat) which used to be most in demand, now both have been superseded by the genetically engineered iceberg – what this lacks in actual earthy flavour is compensated for by its rich texture, crispness and keeping qualities. Courgettes or aubergine slices, fried in olive oil, go beautifully with plain spaghetti and tomato sauce, and the young, tender courgette flowers make exquisite fritters. Cauliflower and spinach go into our famous Torta tal-Lampuki. Seasons, on the whole, are short and there are different ways of cooking vegetables, according to whether they are young and tender or large and tending to be coarse.

Many vegetables do not suffer from being prepared in advance when there are a lot of preparations to be made. Boil or poach them in the usual way but remove them when they are 'al dente' and plunge them into very cold water (as you would hard-boiled eggs) to stop the cooking process. Drain and set aside. When the time comes to serve the vegetables, toss them over a low flame with a knob of butter, or fry (depending on the vegetable) until hot and just tender. In this way colour, texture and flavour are all maintained. We do not, however, recommend that ALL vegetables need preliminary blanching, since many can be cooked directly in butter or lemon juice, for example, without coming into contact with water at all.

Try rocket (eruka or Aruka – *eruca sativa*) in your salad or pile it into a fresh bread and butter sandwich – but, be warned, it might be an aphrodisiac if this old Latin saying is to be believed 'Tardos ad venerem excitat eruca maritos'. Young broad beans with both outer pod and inner shells removed accompany fresh gbejniet and crusy bread – black crust, bright pale green and pure white make this an irresistible combination. As children we used to love to nibble raw chick peas (ċiċri-tal-qatta) and Ħobbejża (mallow) – do children in the 1990s enjoy them too? Remember to use fresh herbs – Malta and Gozo have an abundance of them and some (eg fidloqqom (borage – *borago officinalis*); plejju (pennyroyal – *menta pulegium*) sagħtar (Mediterranean wild thyme – *Coridothymus capitatus*) and rignu (oregano – *origanum vulgare*) grow wild. Basil – (*ocimum basilcum*) can now be bought in large bunches. There used to be a tradition until comparatively recently that a pot of basil (Ħabaq) placed on the projecting stone bracket beneath a noticeable window indicated a nubile daughter in the house.

We both spent some of our growing years in Sliema in the days when one woke to the sounds of cocks crowing early in the morning in many town gardens since it was not unusual to keep chickens. Another early morning sound, along with the church bells, was that of donkeys and carts trundling through the streets at dawn bringing in fresh fruit and vegetables from the countryside.

Such sounds would begin at about 4 a.m. so that the produce would be ready for sale when good women returning home from the 5 or 6 a.m. mass could buy their fresh eggs and vegetables from traders who set up stalls near the churches. This would happen in towns and villages all over the islands. Another common and impressive sight was that of dignified, straight-backed, barefoot women walking into the towns carrying baskets of eggs and other produce on their heads, for sale from door to door. They usually represented a producers' co-operative. A little later in the morning one would hear the cries of fish and *rikotta* sellers, then the horse and cart which pulled the bread van, with Good Bread (in English) painted on the side while the baker called out 'ħobż!'. The paraffin sellers would follow, also with donkey and cart, in the early afternoons doing a brisk trade when paraffin (pitrolju) was relied on (for cooking) much more than it is now. On

Wednesdays and Fridays in particular one would hear the call of the fish sellers 'Friski u ħajjin' (fresh and alive!)

Now the donkey and cart have given way to the vegetable vans which one finds all over the island, situated at the street corners till as late as 7.30 p.m. People huddle round in the dark on cold wet winter evenings, patiently waiting their turns while inspecting the vegetables for sale and carrying on a dialogue with one another, and the seller, about the quality of the produce and its suitability for baking or stuffing. As you walk round the corners, in the windy streets of Sliema which lead down to the sea, you will notice not only the distinct smell of the sea but also that of absolutely fresh onions, garlic and leeks, organically grown spinach, huge cauliflowers and shiny purple and tender kohl rabi – used in soups or eaten raw to accompany fresh bread and cheese. You will see enormous bright orange and pale yellow pumpkins (qara-ahmar and qara-Tork) for minestra, and the small, egg-shaped, pale green qarabagħli. In the summer the vans are loaded with bright red, flat or plum-shaped tomatoes, and deep purple aubergines. Look out also for Bambinella – miniature juicy pears and, of course, the most tempting of all fruits – dusky purple, or pale green figs. Some van sellers also sell capers in old jam jars, Malta honey (not always the real thing) and might also take orders for rabbits.

Some things do not change. Henry Teonge, a vicar who visited Malta in the 17th century notes in his diary on 15th January 1676: 'And here in Malta (which was very strange to me) at this time of the year, we bought radishes, cabidges and excellent colly flowers and large ones for 1d per piece'.

Qaqoċċ mimli
Stuffed artichokes

4 globes artichokes
Squeeze of lemon juice
Salt and pepper
2–3 tbsp olive oil

For the stuffing
4 heaped tbsp fresh white bread crumbs
2–3 anchovy fillets, chopped
2–4 cloves garlic, crushed
1–2 tbsp parsley, chopped
1 tbsp black olives, stones and chopped

◆ Soak the artichokes in plenty of water together with a squeeze of lemon juice to preserve their colour.

Break off and discard the small outer leaves, and trim the stalk. (If they are not too tough, the stalks can be peeled, boiled and eaten as a vegetable.) Open out the artichokes by flattening them gently on to the chopping board thus making space between the leaves to hold the stuffing. Some cooks trim the tops off the leaves using scissors.

Mix the stuffing ingredients in a bowl. Take a small quantity at a time and push it with a teaspoon and your clean fingers between the leaves, pushing well down and distributing it evenly around.

Put the prepared artichokes in a sauté pan or saucepan that will hold them upright with little space to spare. Pour about 250 ml water into the bottom of the pan. Pour the oil over the artichokes and sprinkle with salt and pepper. Bring to a boil, cover tightly and simmer for about 45 minutes or until a leaf from the outer edge can be pulled out easily. The vegetables are in fact being steamed. Were the water to be too deep or boil too vigorously, the stuffing would be dissipated. Serve with a dressing of olive oil and lemon juice.

Qlub tal-qaqoċċ 'la torka'

Turkish-style artichoke hearts

8 medium globe artichokes
2–4 tbsp olive oil
2–3 cloves garlic, crushed
Salt and pepper
Juice of ½ lemon
2 tbsp parsley, or basil, finely chopped

◆ Soak the raw globes upside down in salted water for 1 hour. Remove the stalk and break off the outer ranks of coarse leaves, leaving only those pale inner leaves that can mostly be eaten in their entirety. Using a sharp, stainless steel knife, cut off the upper parts of the leaves which remain. Trim and pare the base, removing any roughness or outer skin. Take care to rub any cut surface with a lemon, or dip it in vinegar, to stop discolouration. Part the remaining leaves in the centre with your finger and excavate the choke with a teaspoon or short, sharp knife. Cut each heart into two. Leave in a bowl of acidulated water until ready to cook.

When they are all prepared, place them in a small saucepan. Add the oil, garlic, salt and pepper, 2 tbsp of water and lemon juice. Simmer, tightly covered, over low heat for 20–30 minutes. Sprinkle with chopped fresh parsley or basil and serve hot or cold with good, crusty bread.

Qlub tal-qaqoċċ mimlijin

Stuffed artichoke hearts

8 globe artichokes
250 ml béchamel sauce
100 g ham, chopped (optional)
2 hard-boiled eggs (optional)
1 onion, chopped (optional)
1 tbsp olive oil
1 tbsp Parmesan, grated

◆ Prepare the hearts as in the previous recipe, but do not cut them in half. Simmer until tender, drain and reserve. Prepare a stuffing by cooking a thick béchamel sauce and adding either the ham, hard-boiled eggs, or onion that has been sweated in olive oil, together with the cheese and seasoning. Pile this into the hearts and place under a moderate grill or in an oven at 180°C/350°F/gas 4 until heated through.

Qlub tal-qaqoċċ bil-fwied u l-majjal

Artichoke hearts stuffed with chicken livers and pork

4 globe artichokes
1 large onion, finely chopped
2 tbsp olive oil
200 g minced lean pork
125 ml white wine
125 ml stock or water
100 g chicken livers
Salt and pepper
4 slices white bread, crusts removed
8 tbsp olive oil
1 tbsp chopped parsley

◆ Prepare the artichoke hearts as in the previous recipes, leaving them whole. Stew gently until just tender, 20–25 minutes, drain and resene. Sweat the chopped onion in olive oil until just beginning to take colour. Add the minced pork and cook, moistening at intervals with a mixture of the wine and water or stock. When the pork is almost cooked add the chopped chicken livers, salt and pepper and cook for just five more minutes adding more liquid if necessary. Fill the hearts with this mixture, reserving some of the liquid. Fry the slices of bread in olive oil, until golden. Place a filled artichoke on each slice and pour a little of the reserved liquid on top. Sprinkle with chopped parsley and serve hot.

Stuffat tal-qaqoċċ bil-ful u piżelli

Stewed artichoke hearts with beans and peas

1 cup each of shelled peas and young broad beans
6 large globe artichokes
4 onions, sliced
2 tbsp olive oil
600 g tomatoes, skinned
2–3 cloves garlic, crushed
1 tbsp basil or marjoram, chopped
Salt and pepper

◆ Shell the peas and beans. Remove the skins of each broad bean. Prepare the artichoke hearts as in previous recipes. Reserve in acidulated water.

Make a *taqlija* (literally a 'frying') of the onions in the olive oil until pale golden. Add the garlic, tomatoes and herbs. Simmer to combine, but do not reduce. Add the hearts and simmer for 25–30 minutes. When they are almost done, add the beans and peas and cook until tender. Adjust the seasoning and serve hot or cold.

Fritturi tal-qaqoċċ
Artichoke heart fritters

8 large artichokes.
2 large eggs
1–2tbsp parsley, chopped
Salt and pepper

Olive oil for deep frying

◆ Prepare and cook the artichoke hearts as In the previous recipes. Cut each heart into four neat slices.

Separate the eggs. Beat the whites until stiff, fold in the yolks, the parsley and seasoning.

Dip the artichoke into this batter and fry until brown in deep olive oil. Serve hot with lemon wedges, crusty bread and a salad.

Fritturi tal-artiċokks
Jerusalem artichoke fritters

400–500 g Jerusalem artichokes
1 or 2 eggs, beaten
4 tbsp fresh bread crumbs or galletti *crumbs*
Sunflower or olive oil for frying

◆ Peel the Jerusalem artichokes, keeping them in cold water acidulated with lemon juice or vinegar to preserve their colour until ready to cook. Boil them until tender, drain and cut in half. Cool. Dip into beaten egg, then bread crumbs and fry until golden in shallow or deep oil.

Artiċokks fil-kazzola
Stewed Jerusalem artichokes

800–1000g Jerusalem artichokes
2 tbsp olive oil
2 cloves garlic, crushed
2 tbsp chopped parsley
Juice of half a lemon
Salt and pepper

◆ A delicious vegetable, rich in mineral elements, particularly potassium.

Prepare the Jerusalem artichokes as detailed in the preceding recipe. Drain, then dress while still hot with the garlic, parsley, olive oil, salt and pepper. Serve hot or cold.

Another excellent method is to cook them in the same way as smothered potatoes (page 162) but make sure you have sufficient water as they take longer to cook than potatoes and they may dry out.

Briġiel mimli

Stuffed aubergines

3 large aubergines
1 onion, chopped
2 cloves garlic, crushed
2 tsp tomato purée
300 g minced pork or a mixture of pork and beef
1 tbsp Parmesan cheese, grated
2 eggs, beaten
1 tbsp olive oil and a little butter
Salt and pepper
Fresh bread crumbs or galletti *crumbs or semolina*
50 g butter

◆ Parboil the whole aubergines for 10 minutes. Drain. Cut each one in half lengthwise and scoop out the pulp, leaving a border of about 6 mm. Retain the pulp.

Fry the chopped onion in the oil, add the garlic, tomato purée, the meat and about half the aubergine pulp. Cook for about 15 minutes, until the meat is done, stirring from time to time. Allow to get almost cold; add the eggs, cheese, salt and pepper. Stuff the aubergine shells with this mixture. Top with crumbs or semolina and dot with butter. Bake at 200°C/ 400°F/gas 6 for 30 minutes.

It is possible to make this more substantial by cooking the aubergines on a bed of sliced potatoes and onions described in the method for roasting beef (page 91). Start the potatoes about 45 minutes before the aubergines.

Briġiel u bżar biz-zalza pikkanti

Aubergine and peppers in a piquant sauce

1 large aubergine
6 peppers (capsicums)
6 tbs olive oil
Salt and pepper
250 ml piquant sauce (page 217)

◆ Peel and cut the aubergine into slices about 5 mm thick and sprinkle these with salt. Leave, weighted down in a colander for 1 hour to drain the bitter juices and reduce absorption of fat. Dry the slices on kitchen paper. Cut the peppers in half and remove the seeds. Heat the oil in a heavy pan and fry the vegetables until they are tender. Stir to prevent sticking. Place in a serving dish and cover with the piquant sauce. Good both hot and cold.

Fritturi tal-brinġiel
Aubergine fritters

2 large or 4 small aubergines
Salt
1–2 eggs, beaten
Olive oil for frying

◆ Peel the aubergines and cut each one in half lengthwise. Cut into 3 mm slices. Salt and drain and pat dry as in the previous recipe. Dip in egg and fry in shallow oil until golden on both sides. Dry on more kitchen paper and serve hot with pasta dishes. They go well with spaghetti with tomato sauce.

Brinġiel argodolce
Sweet and sour aubergines

2 large aubergines
2 tbsp olive oil
6 cloves garlic, chopped4
tomatoes, peeled and chopped
1 tsp fresh mint
2 tsp sugar
3 tsp wine vinegar

◆ Peel the aubergines and cut into dice. Salt, drain and pat dry as in preceding recipes. Fry in the oil, stirring constantly. Add the garlic and, a little while later, the tomatoes. Cover and simmer for half an hour. Remove from the heat and stir in the sugar, mint and vinegar. Correct the seasoning. Serve cold.

Forma tal-brinġiel
Aubergine mould

4 medium aubergines
Olive oil for frying
1 onion, chopped
3 or more cloves garlic, crushed
600 g tomatoes
1 tbsp fresh basil, chopped
1 tsp sugar
Salt and pepper
4–6 tbsp grated Parmesan
4–5 eggs, beaten

◆ This is one of our favourite dishes and never fails to please. It is probably best eaten cold

Peel then cut the aubergine into slices about 3 mm thick. Salt, drain and dry as in the previous recipes. Fry until golden in hot olive oil and drain again on kitchen paper. Reserve.

Soften the onion in olive oil Add the garlic, then the tomatoes, basil, sugar, salt and pepper and simmer until thick. Check the seasoning and reserve.

Oil a large pudding basin. Fill it in layers, starting with tomato sauce, then aubergines, followed by a little grated cheese and beaten egg. Continue until the basin is three quarters full, finishing with tomato sauce. You must leave space as the eggs will rise. Cover the basin with greaseproof, foil or its own lid and steam, in a large covered saucepan with the water no more than halfway up the sides of the basin, until set, for approximately 45 minutes. Ensure the saucepan does not boil dry.

If you like to reduce the amount of oil (aubergines absorb a great deal), it is possible to poach some of the aubergine slices in stock. or fry them in a non-stick pan.
Courgettes or *qarabȧgħli* can also be used, instead of the aubergine.

Pastizzotti tal-bringiel

Aubergine tartlets

2 large aubergines
1 medium onion, sliced
1 tbsp olive oil
3 cloves garlic, crushed
2 tomatoes, peeled and chopped
Salt and pepper
Shortcrust or puff pastry (made with 200 g flour)
2 hard-boiled eggs, sliced
6 anchovies
Eggs for glazing

◆ Peel, dice, salt, drain and dry the aubergines, as before. Fry the onion in the oil until soft, add the garlic and cook some more, then the tomatoes and aubergines. Simmer until the aubergines are cooked. Season with pepper and a little salt. Leave to cool.

Roll out the pastry and cut out circles to fit greased tartlet tins, leaving sufficient for lids. Spoon some mixture into each tartlet, add a slice of hard-boiled egg and a small cross of anchovy, then a little more aubergine. Cut out more circles of pastry, moisten the edges and cover the the tartlets. Brush with a little beaten egg. Bake at 200°C/400°F/gas 6 for 15 minutes, then 180°C/350°F/gas 4 for 15 minutes.

The same ingredients can be used to make one large pie. Another version does not include the anchovies suggested here. Instead, approximately 100 g of minced pork is fried with the onions and garlic before adding the tomatoes and aubergines. The filling is bound with 2 beaten eggs which are folded in before the tarlets are filled.

Ful tan-nanna

Grandmother's broad beans

1.5 kg fresh broad beans
1 onion, sliced
2 tbsp olive oil
2 tsp tomato purée
3 slices white bread
2 tbsp wine vinegar
2 cloves garlic, crushed
2 tbsp mint chopped
Salt and pepper

◆ Shell the broad beans and remove the crescent shaped piece on the top of each bean. Fry the onion in the oil until soft and golden. Add the tomato purée, then the beans, and enough water to come half way up the pot. Season with salt and pepper. Simmer until the beans are tender. Soak the bread in the vinegar, squeeze out any surplus and mash with a fork. Add the garlic and mint. Stir this mixture into the cooked beans. Serve hot.

Ful bit-tewm

Beans with garlic

1.25 kg broad beans
2–6 cloves garlic
1 tbsp chopped parsley
1 tbsp wine vinegar
2 tbsp olive oil
Salt and pepper

◆ Remove the outer pods and the inner skins of the beans. Put them in a saucepan and add the crushed or whole garlic. Two cloves is the minimum to make this a well-flavoured dish. Add the other ingredients together with about 250 ml water. Simmer slowly until beans are cooked. Serve hot or cold.

Ful imgiddem

Bitten beans

1.25 kg broad beans
2 tbsp olive oil
2 cloves garlic, chopped
Salt and pepper
1 tbsp tomato purée
2–3 tbsp fresh white bread crumbs
1 tbsp chopped fresh parsley

◆ This may be made when the beans have reached the end of their season when they are large and rather tough. Remove both pods and inner skins. Sweat the garlic in oil without colouring. Add the beans and enough water to cover comfortably. The beans should not be stirred during cooking, so that they do not mash or break up. Add seasoning and tomato purée. Cover and simmer until tender, add the bread crumbs and parsley and a little more crushed raw garlic if liked. Serve hot or cold.

Bigilla

400 g dried broad beans
2 tbsp olive oil
1 head of garlic, crushed
1 red chilli pepper, finely chopped
1 tbsp mixed fresh marjoram, mint or basil
Salt
Olive oil

◆ This is very much a country dish. In Malta, the beans are bought from forage merchants, not delicatessens. The *bigilla* seller used to be a familiar, comforting figure in village streets on cold winter nights. The dish is now making a comeback and can be found at *salumerie* and at the market in Valletta. At least one restaurant serves it regularly, as a first course, accompanied by garlic bread.

Wash the beans and soak for a few hours or overnight in cold water. Bring to the boil in the same water, omitting salt at this stage. Simmer until the beans are very tender and the water has evaporated. Mash the beans roughly. Turn on to a serving dish and add all the other ingredients to taste. Pour a little extra oil over the top. To reduce the heat of chilli, remove some or most of the seeds.

Kaboċċa mimlija bl-rikotta

Cabbage leaves stuffed with rikotta

1 medium young cabbage
200 g rikotta
2 eggs, beaten
1 tbsp Parmesan, grated
A few sultanas
Salt and pepper
3 tbsp olive oil

◆ Separate the leaves from the stalk of the cabbage and blanch them in salted boiling water for 2 minutes. Drain and cool. Place them flat on a work surface and remove any tough ribs. Combine the *rikotta*, eggs, cheese, sultanas, salt and pepper. Put a teaspoon of this stuffing at one end of a leaf and roll up. The stuffing will expand during cooking. Heat the oil in a heavy saucepan, place the cabbage leaf rolls carefully on the bottom, cover the pan and cook over a gentle heat until the filling is set and the cabbage tender. Accompany with hot tomato sauce as described on page 216.

Kaboċċa mimlija bil laħam

Cabbage stuffed with minced meat

1 medium cabbage
1 onion, chopped
400 g minced beef and pork
1 tsp tomato purée
1 tbsp Parmesan, grated
2 eggs, beaten
Salt and pepper
4 tbsp olive oil

◆ Pull the cabbage leaves off the stalk and cut away any tough ribs. Place the leaves in a large bowl and pour boiling water over them, cover with a cloth or plate and leave to soften for about 5 minutes. Drain and cool.

Fry the onion until golden in 1 tbsp of oil. Add the meat then the tomato purée. Cook, stirring from time to time, for about 10 minutes. Remove from the heat and add the cheese, eggs, salt and pepper. Use this mixture to stuff the cabbage leaves, as before. Cook with some oil in a heavy saucepan as detailed in the previous recipe. This version need not be accompanied by tomato sauce. Boiled or mashed potatoes or rice would go well.

Kaboċċa bil-bacon

Cabbage with bacon

1 small cabbage
4 rashers smoked bacon, chopped
1 tbsp olive oil
Freshly ground black pepper

◆ Shred the cabbage finely and cook in boiling salted water until just tender. Drain. Fry the bacon in a heavy pan until it begins to take colour, using a little olive oil or good dripping if the bacon is lean. Add the cabbage and stir until it is heated through, on a fairly high heat. Season with pepper and serve very hot to accompany meat dishes. A simple but popular dish. It has been known to accompany the turkey on Christmas Day.

Fritturi tal-pastard

Cauliflower fritters

1 cauliflower, in florets
2 eggs
Chopped parsley
Olive oil for shallow frying
Salt and pepper

◆ Boil the florets until just tender in salted water. Plunge them in cold water to stop the cooking. Drain. Separate the eggs and beat the yolks lightly. Beat the whites until stiff but not dry. Fold the yolks in; add the parsley. Dip the cauliflower in the batter and fry in shallow oil until golden. Serve with lemon wedges and sprinkle on the salt and pepper. These go well with brain fritters (page 110).

Stuffat tal-pastard

Cauliflower stew

1 onion, sliced
1 tbsp olive oil
1 tbsp tomato purée
250 ml stock or water
1 cauliflower, cut into 8
1 tbsp sultanas
8 stoned and chopped black olives
Salt and pepper

◆ Fry the onion lightly, in oil in a heavy saucepan, until soft. Add the tomato purée and cook, stirring occasionally, for a few minutes more. Add all the other ingredients, being careful not to add too much stock at this stage. Simmer for about 20 minutes until the cauliflower is cooked. Add more stock or water if the mixture tends to stick, but the final dish should be fairly dry. You may like to add up to 1 tsp of sugar.

Qarabagħli mimli bil-laħam

Courgettes or qarabagħli stuffed with meat

800 g large qarabaghli *or courgettes*
1 onion, chopped
1 tbsp olive oil
2 large ripe tomatoes, peeled, deseeded and chopped, or 2 heapted tsp tomato purée
600 g minced beef
2 eggs, beaten
2 tbsp Parmesan, grated
Salt and pepper
Fresh white bread crumbs, or semolina

◆ *Qarabagħli 'Cucurbita Pepo – Cucurbitaceae* family' is probably the most popular vegetable in Malta, perhaps because it is so versatile. It is a small, round summer squash or marrow. When they are new and very tender, each vegetable the size of a small egg and a light green colour, it is best to boil them briskly in an uncovered pan and serve them hot with a little olive oil and a squeeze of lemon. Take care to avoid overcooking them so the colour and excellent flavour are retained. As the season progresses, the *qarabagħli* increase in girth until the size of large oranges. Medium specimens can be used in stews or cut into rounds and fried to go with pasta dishes. Finally, they begin to take on a pale and dull appearance, making a very good thick soup, or they can be stuffed as in this recipe.

'Several varieties of marrows are available in Europe and, as Stobart (see Bibliography) reminds us there are huge differences between varieties of the same species. In England qarabagħli can be found in areas which have Cypriot communities. Their name in Turkish is 'beyaz kabak' and in Greek 'koloythia'. If qarabagħli are not available courgettes or zucchini may be substituted. The watery vegetable marrow grown to giant dimensions by English gardeners is not a satisfactory alternative as its flavour is much less delicate.

Parboil the *qarabagħli* in boiling water for 10 minutes. Drain them and cut each one in half, scoop out the insides with a teaspoon and reserve about half the pulp.

Fry the onion in the oil until soft. Add the tomatoes and cook for a further few minutes. Add the beef and cook until done. Stir in the marrow pulp, then allow to cool. Add the eggs, cheese and seasoning to this mixture. Fill the marrow halves and sprinkle with bread crumbs or semolina. Place in a lightly oiled baking dish. Pour over a little more oil or dot with butter. Bake at 180°C/350°F/gas 4 until thoroughly heated and browned on top, 30–45 minutes. To make this a more substantial dish, bake it on a bed of potatoes and sliced onions as suggested in the recipe for roast beef (page 91), adjusting times accordingly.

Qara' twil mimli

Stuffed gourd

800 g qara' twil
400 g minced beef and pork
1 tbsp onion, grated
2 eggs, beaten
Salt and pepper
500 ml tomato sauce (page 191)

◆ The species is *Trichosanthes Cucumerina* which also includes the Melon family. Goode and Wilson (see bibliography) describe them as 'fruit growing like a giant sausage up to 60cm long when mature. Related species are harvested from places as remote from one other as Papua New Guinea (known as the New Guinea Bean) and South America (known as Club or Viper Gourd.) This gourd is translated in Busuttil's dictionary of 1964 as a 'long pumpkin or trumpet gourd'. It is stuffed in a similar fashion to the *qarabagħli*, although our recipe suggests different ingredients for the stuffing.

Cut the *qara' twil* into 5 cm lengths and carefully scoop out the pulp so that you have a cup shape. Mix the meat, onion and beaten eggs together, season, then fill the cups. Heat the tomato sauce and stand the filled gourd in it. Cover and simmer slowly for approximately 45 minutes. Serve very hot. 'A variation it to stuff the *qara twil* with *rikotta*. For a smallish gourd use approximately 100 to 150g *rikotta*, mixed with a large beaten egg, freshly grated parmesan, salt and pepper and freshly chopped parsley. Follow the same method as above.

Ċentinarja
Chayote

◆ Centinarja (*Sechium Edule*) is a less popular vegetable because it is extremely hard when raw and very difficult to peel. However, it is delicious and more like potato in texture. Peel with a good potato peeler. It may be boiled and eaten hot or cold with olive oil or butter, or it may be braised or stewed. Note that *qara twil* and *centinarja* are gourds and of a different species from marrows, pumpkins and squashes.

Qarabagħli mimli bl-irkotta
Qarabagħli or courgettes stuffed with Rikotta

800 g medium qarabagħli *or courgettes*
200 g rikotta
2 eggs, beaten
1 tbsp Parmesan, grated
2 onions, sliced

◆ If using round *qarabagħli* or a similar small summer squash, top and tail, setting aside the slice from the top to use as a lid. If using large courgettes, wipe, trim, and split in half lengthwise. Remove the pulp, leaving a cup or a boat to fill. Reserve the pulp.

Beat the *rikotta* to make sure it is smooth. Add the eggs, Parmesan and seasoning. Stuff the *qarabagħli* with this mixture; do not overfill as the eggs expand. Cover each one with its own lid.

Place the onions and the marrow pulp in a

50 g butter and a little olive oil
2 tsp tomato puree
2 tsp sugar
1 tsp vinegar

large saucepan. Add the butter and oil and 2 tbsp water. Stand the qarabaghli closely together on top of the vegetables and cover tightly. Simmer for about 45 minutes until the *qarabagħli* are cooked.

Lift the marrows on to a serving dish and finish the sauce. Add the tomato purée to the onion and simmer for about 15 minutes, stirring occasionally. Remove from the heat, add the vinegar and sugar and correct the seasoning. Pour this sauce over the vegetables and serve very hot. This is typical of the thrift of the Maltese and Gozitan cook: the pulp is not discarded but used to thicken the sauce.

Qarabagħli biz-zalza pikkanti

Qarabagħli or courgettes with piquant sauce

800 g qarabagħli *or courgettes*
250 ml piquant sauce (page 217)

◆ Wash and dry the *qarabagħli* or courgettes and cut into slices about 6 mm thick. Heat a generous amount of olive oil in a heavy frying pan and fry them until golden on both sides. Dry on kitchen paper. Arrange in a suitable dish, either making layers of *qarabaghlı* and sauce, or just pour the sauce over the top. Serve cold.

Fritturi tal-fjur tal-qarabagħli

Qarabagħli or courgette flower fritters

◆ Just as the Italians make fritters of courgette flowers, so do the Maltese of their *qarabagħli*. Remove the hard core from each flower and dip in an egg and parsley batter prepared as for brain fritters (page 110). Fry in deep olive oil until golden. Serve very hot.

Stuffat tal-qarabagħli

Casserole of qarabagħli or courgettes

600 g medium qarabagħli *or courgettes*
3 onions, sliced
2 large tomatoes, peeled and sliced
2 cloves garlic, crushed
1 tbsp marjoram
3 tbsp olive oil
2 tbsp water
Salt and pepper

◆ Wipe and slice the *qarabagħli* or courgettes in 6 mm slices. Arrange all the vegetables in a heavy saucepan; season and add the marjoram. Add the oil and water, cover and simmer until tender. Do not add too much water as the *qarabagħli* produce a lot of moisture while cooking. Add a little more oil at the table if liked.

Stuffat tal-qara-aħmar

Pumpkin stew

2 onions, chopped
2 tbsp olive oil
2 cloves garlic, crushed
400 g pumpkin, peeled, chopped and the seeds removed
Salt and pepper
2 tbsp of sultanas
2 tbsp water

◆ Cook the onion in olive oil until very soft but not brown. Add the garlic and cook a little longer. Add the pumpkin and stir, allowing it to take colour. Season. Add the sultanas and a very little water. Cover, and simmer for 15–20 minutes. Serve with rice and a green vegetable.

Indivja straċċnata

Curly endive

1 large curly endive
2 tbsp olive oil
4 or more cloves garlic, crushed

◆ Wash the endive well, and blanch in boiling salted water until limp. Drain and chop the leaves. Stir-fry them in hot olive oil with crushed garlic.

The blanching water is considered to be a very healthy drink. It may be sharpened with a little lemon juice. Drink it hot.

Indivja mimlija
Stuffed Curly Endive

1 large curly endive
4 heaped tbsp fresh white bread crumbs
1–2 tbsp parsley, chopped
2–3 anchovy fillets, chopped
2 cloves garlic, crushed
1 tbsp black olives, stoned and chopped
Salt and pepper
3 tbsp olive oil

◆ Wash the endive and blanch the leaves in boiling salted water. Drain and cool. Combine all the other ingredients, except the olive oil. Lay the leaves flat on a work surface. Put some of the stuffing on one end of each leaf and roll into a neat package. Place the rolls in a saucepan with the olive oil at the base and simmer, covered, until tender.

Bżar aħdar mimli
Stuffed sweet peppers

1 sweet pepper per person
200 g fresh bread crumbs
75 g anchovy fillets, chopped
8 black olives, stoned and chopped
1 tbsp capers, chopped
1 tbsp fresh herbs, chopped (basil, mint or parsley)
Salt and pepper
Olive oil

◆ The amount of stuffing should be enough for 2–3 peppers (red, green or yellow peppers can be used). The peppers may be left whole or cut in half horizontally. In either case, remove the seeds. Mix all the stuffing ingredients together. Stuff the peppers and place them in an oiled baking dish, pour more olive oil over them and bake at 180°C/350°F/gas 4 for about 40 minutes. Eat hot or cold.

Bżar aħdar mimli bil-laħam

Peppers stuffed with meat and rice

1 sweet pepper per person
1 onion, chopped
2 cloves garlic, crushed
2 tbsp olive oil
400 g minced beef, pork or lamb
2 tomatoes peeled, chopped, and deseeded or 2 tsp tomato purée
4 tbsp cooked rice
2 eggs, beaten
2 tbsp Parmesan, grated
½ freshly ground nutmeg and cinnamon
Salt and pepper

◆ Prepare the peppers as before. The quantity for the filling is, again, for 2–3 people. Fry the chopped onion and garlic in olive oil until golden, add the meat and brown it, then add the tomatoes or puree and cook for a few minutes more. Let cool. Mix in the boiled rice, Parmesan, beaten eggs, spices and seasoning. The rice should be firm and slightly undercooked. Bake as in the previous recipe and serve hot with a good tomato sauce. Similar recipes in Middle Eastern cookery books include a few sultanas and nuts. You may like to try this addition.

Bżar aħdar mixwi

Grilled peppers

One sweet pepper per person
Olive oil
Garlic, crushed
Basil, parsley or mint, chopped
Salt and pepper

◆ Wash and dry the peppers. Leave whole. Grill under a very hot grill on all sides until the skins blacken and blister. Wrap in a tea towel or kitchen paper until cool. Peel off the skin; remove the seeds. Slice thinly lengthwise. Dress with plenty of olive oil, crushed garlic and herbs. Season liberally. This is truly a favourite and can be eaten in a number of ways. When grills were not available people would turn the peppers on the lid of a biscuit tin placed over a gas burner. The result was as good. However, the best way is over charcoal.

Basal għad-dobbu

Onions stewed in wine with fresh herbs

800 g medium onions
375 ml red wine
2 sprigs fresh parsley
2 sprigs fresh rosemary
2 bay leaves
8 peppercorns, lightly crushed
Salt
2 tbsp olive oil

◆ Slice the onions thinly and place in a heavy saucepan with all the other ingredients. Cover and cook gently until the onions are tender. This dish makes a delicious light lunch or supper, with fresh bread, or it may accompany other dishes.

Torta ta'l-ispinaċi

Spinach pie

For the pastry
600 g plain flour
a pinch of salt
7 tbsp olive oil and sunflower oil, mixed
6–8 tbsp cold water
Egg, beaten, or milk, to glaze

For the filling
1.5 kg spinach
1 onion, chopped
2 tbsp olive oil
8 black olives, stoned and chopped
2 tins anchovy fillets
100 g cooked fresh peas

◆ This quantity will make two shallow pies approximately 15–18 cm across.

Sieve the flour into a bowl with the salt. Mix the oil with 2 thsp water and add to the flour. Bring together with the rest of the water until you have a pliable consistency. Put to rest in the refrigerator.

Wash the spinach and cook. Drain and cool. Soften the onion in olive oil; add the olives and spinach and fry for a few minutes more. Add the peas and the anchovy fillets. Remove from the heat and allow to cool.

Roll out the pastry and line the greased pie dishes, leaving sufficient for the lids. Spoon in the filling and cover with the rest of the pastry. Make a tiny incision in the centre to allow the steam to escape. Glaze with egg or milk. Cook at 200°C/400°F/gas 6 for 15 minutes. Reduce the heat to 180°C/350°F/gas 4 and cook for 30 minutes more. If you are using two oven shelves, change the position of the pies halfway through the cooking time. Spinach pie is delicious hot or cold.

Tadam mimli

Stuffed tomatoes (1)

6 large tomatoes
4 tbsp fresh white bread crumbs
2 tbsp parsley and mint, chopped
4 anchovy fillets, chopped
4 cloves garlic, crushed
6 black olives, stoned and chopped
Salt and pepper
2–3 tbsp olive oil

◆ This dish may be eaten hot or cold. The best tomatoes are the flat, baking fruit (called in Britain 'beefsteak') and are always most flavoursome when ripened by the summer sun. To eat cold, peel the tomatoes, cut them in half horizontally, scoop out the seeds, sprinkle the insides with a little salt and leave them upside-down to drain. Combine the other ingredients, except the olive oil, and fill the tomato halves. Arrange in a dish, pour some olive oil over each one and chill, but remove from the refrigerator about 30 minutes before eating.

For the hot version, proceed as before. Place the tomatoes in a metal baking dish, pour on 2–3 tbsp olive oil and bake at 180°C/350°F/gas 4 for 30 minutes until tender and the stuffing golden.

Tadam mimli

Stuffed tomatoes (2)

8 large tomatoes
Sugar
Salt
1 onion, finely chopped
50 g butter
1 rasher bacon, chopped
Giblets from a chicken or 100 g chicken livers, chopped
Pinch of nutmeg
150 g rice
2 tbsp Parmesan, grated
1–2 envelopes saffron
Salt and pepper

◆ Cut the tops off the unpeeled tomatoes, scoop out the seeds and pulp with a teaspoon. Sprinkle the shells with a little sugar and salt. Turn them upside down to drain.

Fry the onion in the butter until soft, add the bacon, the giblets or chicken livers and season with nutmeg. Boil the rice for 10 minutes until just tender, drain and add to the onion mixture. Add the Parmesan and the saffron stamens soaked in a tbsp of boiling water. Season, then stuff the tomatoes. Dot with small pieces of butter. Bake in a moderate oven, 180°C/350°F/gas 4, for about 20 minutes.

Forma tal-piżelli
Green pea pudding

400 g dried green peas, fresh peas towards the end of the season, or frozen peas
1 onion, chopped
50 g butter
200 g pork, finely diced
200 g chicken livers and/or giblets, chopped
2 whole eggs, beaten
2 yolks of egg, beaten
Salt and pepper.

◆ If using dried peas, wash them and soak for a few hours. Cook until tender. Do not add salt while they are cooking. Drain and liquidize to a pulp. Cool. If using fresh or frozen peas, cook, drain, liquidise and cool.

For the sauce, fry the onion in the butter until soft, add the pork and, after 5 minutes, the giblets and/or livers. Simmer for about 5 minutes, add a little stock if it needs moistening.

Add about a quarter of this sauce to the pulped peas and stir in the beaten eggs and yolks. Season. Pour this mixture into a greased pudding basin. Leave about 5 cms space at the top of the bowl for expansion. Cover the basin securely with foil or greaseproof. Steam for about 1 hour in a large, covered saucepan. Ensure that the water is always half-way up the basin. Remove from the saucepan when firm and let stand for about 10 minutes. Reheat the remaining sauce, making sure the meat and livers are cooked. Pour the hot sauce over the mould when you turn it out. Serve with a little rice or a green vegetable.

Fritturi tal-qara aħmar
Pumpkin fritters

400 g pumpkin
2 whole eggs or egg yolks only, beaten
3 tbsp flour
Salt and pepper
Olive oil
Fresh mint, chopped

◆ Peel a large slice of pumpkin and remove the seeds. Cut into neat square or oblong pieces. Mix your flour with salt and pepper. Dip the pumpkin first in the egg, then in the flour. Shallow fry in hot olive oil until golden brown. Sprinkle with mint just before serving.

Torta tal-ħaxix

Rich vegetable pie

For the filling

1 large onion, sliced
2 tbsp olive oil
4 cloves garlic, crushed
2 tsp tomato purée
800 g spinach or curly endive
800 g shelled broad beans, the inner skins removed
400 g shelled peas
3 carrots, sliced
4 artichoke hearts (optional)
5 black olives, stoned and chopped
50 g anchovy fillets, chopped
Salt and pepper

For the pastry

Shortcrust or puff pastry, made with 400 g flour
Beaten egg for glaze

◆ Fry the sliced onion in the olive oil in a large saucepan until golden but not brown. Add the crushed garlic and the tomato purée. Wash and drain the spinach or endive. Chop. Add to the pan, cover and leave until thoroughly wilted. Add the carrots and broad beans (and artichoke hearts if available), and 5 minutes later the peas. When all the vegetables are cooked, add the olives and anchovies. Season. Let cool.

Line a shallow oiled pie dish with half the pastry, spoon in the vegetable mixture and cover with a pastry lid. Glaze with beaten egg, after making a small incision for the steam to escape. Cook at 400°F/200°C/gas 6 for 15–20 minutes. Reduce to 180°C/350°F/gas 4, bake for a further 30 minutes.

Some cooks make this an even more substantial dish by adding 2 quartered lightly hard-boiled eggs to the vegetable mixture.

Ħass, ful u piżelli

Lettuce, beans and peas, stewed

2–3 Cos lettuce
200 g spring onions or young leeks, chopped
800 g broad beans, shelled
400 g peas, shelled
2 cloves garlic, crushed
2–3 tbsp olive oil
125 ml water
Salt and pepper

◆ Wash and dry the lettuce. Chop roughly. Remove the inner skin of each broad bean (unless it is very early in their season). Put all the vegetables in a heavy saucepan and pour on the olive oil and water. Bring to the boil and cook uncovered on a brisk heat until tender. Do not overcook. Season well and serve hot or cold.

Patata fgata
Smothered potatoes

6 large potatoes
2 large onions, sliced
2 cloves garlic, crushed
1 or 2 bay leaves
Fresh herbs, chopped
2 tbsp olive oil
1 tbsp white wine (optional)
Salt and pepper

◆ This is one of the easiest and best ways of cooking potatoes and well liked by everyone who tries it. It is the recipe which has been most used from our first edition, by other cookery writers as well as cooks.

Peel the potatoes. Chop into large irregular shapes, each approximately the same size. Place in a large saucepan with about 5 tbsp water. Add the sliced onions and garlic, herbs and seasoning. Use parsley, chervil, marjoram, basil, or mint. If using oregano, be sparing as it is strong. *In extremis*, use half a teaspoon of dried marjoram, basil or mint. Add the wine and olive oil, mixing all well together. Cover and bring to a boil, then simmer for about 20 minutes when the water will have evaporated and the vegetables will be ready to eat.

Fażola bajda bit-tewm u t-tursin
Dried beans with garlic and parsley

400 g dried white butter or haricot beans
2 tbsp olive oil
1 tbsp white wine vinegar
2 tbsp parsley, chopped
4 cloves garlic, crushed
Grated lemon rind
Salt and freshly ground black or white pepper

◆ Soak the beans. Wash them, then cook in fresh water without salt until tender. Drain and, while still hot, mix thoroughly with all the other ingredients. Season. Serve cold.

You may use other kinds of pulses for this dish, for example green or brown lentils, borlotti beans, black-eye peas, *ful medames* or chick peas. It makes a good first course with fresh bread, or can accompany meat or fish dishes or omelettes. It goes particularly well with tinned tuna fish.

Kapunata
Caponata, Maltese style

1 large aubergine, peeled and cut into cubes or half moons
4 tbsp olive oil
1 onion, finely sliced
3 cloves garlic, crushed
6 red, green or yellow peppers, seeded and cut into strips
1 small stick celery, finely chopped
2 tomatoes, peeled, deseeded, chopped
2 courgettes, or qarabagħli
1 tbsp basil, mint or marjoram, chopped (or a mixture)
Salt and pepper
1 tbsp black olives, stoned and chopped
1 tbsp capers

◆ Caponata is a celebrated Sicilian dish. Salt and drain the aubergine. In a large heavy saucepan, heat the oil and add all the vegetables at once, stirring well to coat them with the oil. Season and add the herbs. If fresh herbs are unobtainable, use no more than a teaspoon of good dried herbs. Cover tightly and cook slowly until all the vegetables are done, adding the olives and capers towards the end. Serve either hot or cold.

Some cooks like to pour tomato sauce over the centre of the mound of vegetables and arrange strips of anchovy all round.

HOBŻ, HOBŻ BIŻ-ŻEJT, ĠOBON, PASTIZZI ETC.

BREAD, CHEESE, PIES AND OTHER DISHES

Our bread has been described as the best in the world – perhaps something of an overstatement since one encounters hundreds of varieties of delicious bread all over the world. The French Pain de Campagne (less well known than the baguette) and the Italian Pugliese (for example) come close to the Malta loaf in appearance, but are not the same when you cut them open and taste them. Greek bread (particularly the kind we have eaten in Corfu), resembles it even more though the shape is usually more like the 'bezzun' one finds in Gozo. This is borne out by Parkinson-Large, (p 38) who tells us that one hundred Rhodian families shared the Knights' exile from Rhodes, bringing with them the recipe for our bread. There are, to this day, families of distinct Rhodian origin in Corfu. The bakery belonging to the Order was situated opposite St Augustine's church in Old Bakery Street in Valletta. One of their most famous galleons, the Santa Anna, even had its own bakery.

Maltese and Gozitan bread has a unique taste and texture. The principle used in the baking is similar, but not identical, to true sourdough bread (the kind San Francisco is famous for) which evolves from a spontaneous lactic acid fermentation of flour and water. Our method is not unlike that which uses 'biga' in Italy – a starter dough to which a little yeast (Saccharomyces Cerevisiae) is added. Each day a portion of the previous day's dough is incorporated into the freshly made dough and it is this which gives the mature and sour flavour to the bread. In many parts of our islands wood ovens are still in use. Production is based on a harmonious process, the mixture is low in salt and no improvers of any kind are used. The bread is baked on the floor of the oven at an extremely high temperature which gives it the dark thick crust and slightly burned and irresistible flavour. The characteristic large holes in the finished loaf are produced by the very long first rising, preceded by slow mixing, and the omission of 'knocking back', which is cutomary in most kinds of bread. This means using the knuckles to knock out the large air bubbles which form in rising dough. The loaves are shaped from the risen dough without interfering with the large bubbles of air inside, thus leaving them to survive as large holes when the bread is baked. We know of one mean ancestor of ours who wanted to make the butter go further and used to instruct his children 'aqbżu it-toqob' (literally 'skip the holes'), when they buttered their bread!

Like so many of the acquisitions of modern civilisation the amazing powers of yeasts are thought to have been discovered in the days of the ancient Egyptians. Wild yeast is everywhere in the air around us. It is carried by insects and birds and causes fermentation to occur when it comes into contact with foods – such as moist grain, mashed potatoes and in the natural sugars present in bananas and other fruit. For a long time the way that yeast worked (causing bubbles of air to aerate and raise a flour and water mixture) mystified scientists who worked hard in attempting to discover the secret of it all; the discovery of the microscope, early in the 17th century brought the mystery to an end – that yeast is a living single cell plant which brings about fermentation by breaking down starch and sugar into carbon dioxide and alcohol. Louis Pasteur was thus able to show that it is not grape juice which causes wine to ferment but the bloom in the skins of the fruit. The *bacteria bulgaris* culture which produces yoghurt works on the same principle. Fermentation has been described by one authority as not dissimilar to alchemy – it brings about an alteration in a perishable food, making it preservable while simultaneously improving its qualities.

The commercial variety of yeast we know today is a by-product of beer making. It is believed that its use was discovered first by the Romans who, in turn, had learned it from their captured German tribes. However, the practice spread widely and overtook pure lactic acid fermentation when, in about 1780, the French government granted brewers a licence to sell their waste product to the bakers. Commercial yeast is potent and can be relied upon to work and to work fast – all factors essential to the large scale production of bread for profit. However, the practice of using mature dough still continues in many parts of the world and nutritionists claim that the consumption of fermented products is beneficial to our health.

The lactic acid fermentation of San Francisco bread goes back to the time of the settlement of the American frontier when a crock or pot of sourdough starter was carried by the trappers and miners. It was a valued possession which could be constantly replenished and passed down from one generation to the next. When the Israelites escaped their captivity in Egypt the practice of leavening bread by fermentation was also taking place but, unlike the American trappers the Israelites' hasty departure caused them to leave their leaven behind. This is recorded in Exodus (xii. 34–39) 'And the people took their dough before it was leavened, their kneading troughs being bound up in their clothes upon their shoulders . . . and they baked unleavened cakes of the dough which they brought forth out of Egypt, for it was not leavened because they were thrust out of Egypt and could not tarry'.

We cannot be sure when the kind of bread we eat in Malta now began to replace the 'pane misturato' (dark and heavy bread made from ground wheat and barley) recorded as late as 1582. (Cassar, p 4) Neither do we know precisely, how and when lactic acid fermentation began to evolve into the kind of slow rising process, with the addition of brewers' yeast, which takes place today. Wherever it remains part of the staple diet bread has not lost the powerful symbolism which is shared by people of all classes. During the hungry years of World War 2 and for a very long time afterwards it came to be regarded as sinful to throw away even the smallest piece of bread.

The fact that our traditional baking industry is now under threat has therefore become a matter of concern. It may not be immediately noticeable but our daily loaf is changing before our eyes. Some of our traditional bakers have begun to abandon the long, time-consuming and labour intensive process which produces our daily bread, in favour of a quicker process which involves the use of various improvers and a dramatic reduction in the rising process. The outside appearance of the Maltese loaf has not changed – that is what is so deceptive – but cut it open and examine it and you will be able to distinguish between the loaf which has been prepared and baked in the traditional way and the one which has not. The first will have a slightly chewy open texture with plenty of uneven holes in the dough; the loaf which has had a quick rising, with the addition of improvers and possibly baked in a steam oven, will look like a cellulose sponge (and almost taste like one too) with only the tiniest of holes, evenly spread. The difference in flavour will be noticeable. Not all bakers have abandoned the old recipes and methods so, depending on where you live, you might still be lucky enough to be getting 'real' bread.

In 1992 the Government gave Medigrain responsibility to monitor the milling of grain and the baking of bread in order to ensure that the characteristics of traditional bread making are preserved. There are 165 bakers in Malta and Gozo and until 1993 80% of them baked bread of the traditional kind. Most of them are small businesses run by one very experienced baker. Our bakers are artists in their craft, they work in the heart of residential districts and have low levels of production. Their work is hard and tiring but the art continues to be passed on to each generation. It is our responsibility and that of our government to ensure that the tradition never dies out. Indeed the price of a traditional loaf might have to rise considerably if bakers are to receive an appropriate return for their talents and hard labour. In other European Countries the slow-fermenting method which had largely been abandoned is now being revived, for those who can afford it. In 1998 a sourdough loaf weighing 1.6 kilos could be delivered to your door by an organic food specialist in London for a cost of approximately £2.50 (sterling).

Here is a recipe you can try at home – we must emphasise that we do not claim for one moment that it will taste as good as the excellent loaf you can buy from a Maltese oven. Apart from anything else no domestic oven can compare with the kind of oven the Maltese and Gozitan bakers use. We give it for those who like to experiment and discover (and perhaps teach their children) as well as for Maltese people living far from home. Beware, bread making can become addictive!

Note: the amount of yeast we indicate is deliberately not very much. Larger amounts of yeast make the dough rise too quickly and adversely affect the flavour of the bread when baked). Provided your yeast is fresh and you leave the dough to rise for long enough and you do not use too hot water your dough will always rise!

Ħobż Malti
Maltese Bread

First stage *100 unbleached (strong flour); 7 g fresh yeast (or the equivalent in easy-blend or dried yeast) 90–100 mls tepid water.*

Second Stage *the large walnut sized dough produced from your first stage (or your earlier baking). This is called* ħmira *or* tinsila. *100 g strong unbleached flour. 90–100 mls tepid water.*

Third Stage *7 g fresh yeast (or the equivalent, as above); 250 mls tepid water; Half the* ħmira *or* tinsila *from the second stage 400 g strong unbleached flour; 1–2 level teaspoons salt. Sesame seeds or additional flour for dusting.*

◆ If you are accustomed to bread making use a piece of uncooked dough, the size of a large walnut (or a little bigger) and proceed to the second stage. Otherwise start at the first stage. Place the flour in a bowl. There is no need to sieve it. Add no salt. If possible use well water or water which has been boiled. The temperature should be roughly blood heat, just cool enough to hold your little finger in it. Cream the fresh yeast with some of the warm water. If using easy blend yeast mix it straight into the flour. Add almost all the remaining water and mix it (by hand as it is such a small amount) until you have a smooth dough, adding more water if it is too dry. Knead it well for a few minutes then place in a bowl, cover with a clean cloth and leave in a warm room or airing cupboard for about 6 hours, though it can be left longer. The temperature should be around 21C or 70F. It can also be left overnight in a cooler temperature.

Now proceed to the second stage. Place the tinsila in the tepid water. Mix in the flour (no salt) and knead into a ball. Cover and leave to rise in the same way as described above.

For the third stage cream the yeast in the water, add one half of the second stage dough (reserve the remainder in fridge or freezer for your next baking). Mix the dough with the yeast and water and dissolve it by squeezing it through your fingers. Add the flour and salt, mix to a dough. Remove to a work surface and knead it for a good ten minutes until it is smooth and pliable. (You may use a mixer or processor but it should not be over-processed). Set it to rise, covered, in a warm place. Sourdough rising should be slow. As you become more confident you will learn to use less yeast and trust the sourdough to raise your bread very slowly. This is what produces the texture and flavour. Leave to rise, covered, for about three hours, and gently turn the dough over twice during this period leaving it in the bowl.

Now return the dough to a floured table – you can remove another piece of dough for future baking. Do not knock back or knead the dough in order that the air bubbles inside can be left intact. Just divide the dough into two or more pieces or leave whole to make one large loaf. Dip the top of the loaf into a mound of sesame seeds or sprinkle with flour. Set it to rise in a warm environment on a greased baking sheet until double in bulk – about 45 minutes. Some bakers turn the loaves face down in the flour and face up again before baking. These loaves acquire a different flavour. The dough will spread sideways, as well as upwards, so use a baking sheet of sufficient size. The bread is baked at 230C; 450F Gas Mark 8 for approximately 30 to 40 minutes. It should be well risen when it goes into the oven – this encourages a solid loaf and irregular holes – a part of the process involved in the original slow mixing. A few bakers like to cut a large cross in the top of the loaf with scissors or a razor. This eliminates the cracks and makes the loaf look larger but tends to be less popular. Check the bread after about 25 minutes and turn them around. If you have made two or more loaves you will notice that they have stuck together – this is intentional. Allow to cool uncovered in order to achieve a crisp crust. Day old bread can be revived by dampening the crust with cold water and placing in a hot oven for 5 to 10 minutes.

We recently learned of another ancient way of storing sour dough starter, from a German Dominican nun who remembers her mother using it on the family farm. Instead of being frozen the lump of dough to be kept was simply left to dry – in time it came to look like a piece of wood. When the time came to use it again, the dry lump was re-constituted with water over a period of a day or two. The mixture was stirred from time to time until it regained softness and pliability and was then used in the usual way.

Ftira
Flat Malta Bread

◆ This is the name given to Maltese bread when it is baked in a round flat disc. One used to have to order them specially but now the bakers produce them at all times.

The *ftira* can be filled most satisfactorily. Split in half horizontally and use the same ingredients we use for *ħobż biż-żeft*. Anchovies always feature in a *ftira*. Press the halves together and leave until ready to eat.

Ħobż biż-żejt
Bread and Oil

Thick slices of fresh Malta bread
*Large ripe tomatoes – the flat or plum shaped varieties are best (*ċatti *or* bżenguli*)*
Olive oil
Coarse salt salt. black pepper

◆ Malta's other national dish, popular as an after-swimming snack with every section of the population (as well as visitors) during the summer. Some of us even like *ħobż biż-żejt* for breakfast. This way of preparing bread and oil resembles the Provençal *pan bagn* and other recipes found in Mediterranean countries.

There are many additions to the simple base sliced onions, crushed garlic, good olives, capers, anchovies and fresh herbs such as basil, mint or marjoram. The *ħobż biż-żejt* obtainable in bars all over the islands (since our book was first published, and for which we claim some of the credit!) now has an invariable addition of tinned tuna fish. This is not authentic but still good. A little wine vinegar may be added too. Use good quality ingredients and no substitutes. Disregard versions which use sliced white bread, and butter instead of oil. A *baguette* is just acceptable as a substitute for Maltese bread.

Cut the tomatoes in half. Remove the seeds if you like. Dip them in olive oil which has been poured into a plate. Rub large slices of bread with the oil and tomato until the bread takes on a pink colour. Leave the pieces of tomato on the bread, cutting them into slightly smaller pieces if very large. If you have been careful with the oil, sprinkle on some more, then add any or all of the other ingredients.

Eat within half an hour of making or the bread will soften. This is not always possible, for instance if you are taking the bread to the beach. In that case, wrap in greaseproof paper or foil and pack into a large box.

Pastizzi
Savoury Cheesecakes

For the pastry
400 g plain flour
½ tspn salt
200 ml cold water (approximately)
125–50 g margarine, lard, butter, or a mixture

For the filling
400 g rikotta
Salt and Pepper
4 eggs, beaten

◆ Few visitors to Malta and Gozo will leave without having tasted *pastizzi*. Many become addicted to them. Although we translate them as 'cheesecakes' they bear no resemblance to the European or English varieties but owe their origin to Sicilian and, previously, Arab sources. *Pastizzi* making is an art. One specialist we spoke to recently said he'd been making *pastizzi* for more than 21 years and still had not attained perfection. We give you these recipes knowing that while they will produce good results they are unlikely to taste as superb as most of those you can buy in the shops. A common sight in Valletta until not very long ago was of young waiters emerging from small bars carrying trays of hot *pastizzi* and tall glass tumblers of tea or coffee for office employees. One famous bar was that of Dimitri Buhagiar in Republic Street, then known as Kingsway.

Pastizzi are almost certainly of Arab origin and the 'roly-poly' method of making pastry is a typical example of their fine culinary tradition. The best way to learn to make *pastizzi* is to watch them being made: in St Paul's or Merchants Street in Valletta, or in Rabat, Hamrun or Msida. However, although many shops sell *pastizzi*, they do not make them on the premises.

We give two recipes for *pastizzi* filled with *rikotta*, but other fillings can also be obtained, such as cooked and mashed dried peas, well seasoned and with a hint of curry powder (that colonial influence again), or with chopped anchovies added to the peas. More recently, a small amount of spinach has sometimes been added to the *rikotta*.

Some people like the plain *rikotta* variety dipped in sugar. Some of the grander cafés in Valletta serve a version of our national snack made with ordinary flaky or puff pastry in round shapes, with lids. We see nothing to recommend them. They don't compare with the authentic version.

To make the pastry, mix the sieved flour and salt with approximately 200 ml of cold water into a soft, pliable but not sticky dough. Knead well. Leave to rest for about an hour.

Make sure that the fat you are going to use is spreadable. Roll, stretch and pull the dough on a floured surface (a long kitchen table) into a long strip or 'rope'. Spread half the fat over the entire length of dough, first with a palette knife, then with clean hands. Take one end of the 'rope' and roll it up like a Swiss roll, but make the rolling somewhat uneven, turning it tightly sometimes, then more loosely. Rest it in the refrigerator.

Repeat the rolling and stretching so that the 'roll' is once more a long strip. Spread the remaining fat. Roll it up again like a Swiss roll, but this time in a different direction from the first roll. All these instructions enhance the flakiness of the finished pastry. Rest it again.

Mash the *rikotta* and salt and pepper. Add the beaten eggs. Cut off pieces of dough the size of a small egg with a sharp knife. Pull out each piece with your fingers until a thin disc. Place a spoonful of the *rikotta* mixture in the centre. Close the dough around it and seal the edge with your fingers. Place on a lightly oiled baking sheet and bake at 200°C/400°F/gas 6 for approximately 25 minutes. Eat hot.

Pastizzi, mark II.

◆ This method (given to us by nuns) results in *pastizzi* of an ornate appearance, and is in some ways similar to recipes encountered in books of Middle Eastern origin, such as the medieval Baghdad cookery book translated by A. J. Arberry.

Use the same ingredients as in the previous recipe, but you may like to double the quantity to make the effort worthwhile.

Divide the flour and water dough into two equal parts, after it has rested for an hour. Divide the total quantity of fat into two parts too. Keep one half of this fat firm as you would for an English pastry recipe.

With the first portion of the dough, and that half of fat that you have kept cool and firm, make a traditional flaky or rough puff pastry. Follow the instructions of your favourite manual. Leave this to rest, wrapped in a butter paper, in the refrigerator.

With the second portion of dough (and the softened fat), roll out as long and thin as possible as in the previous recipe. Spread the fat as before but this time cut the strip into three lengthwise. Roll up one strip very tightly like a Swiss roll. Place it on one end of the second strip and roll again. Place on one end of the third strip of pastry and roll tightly again. Wrap in paper and leave in the refrigerator.

Prepare the *rikotta* filling as before. To make the *pastizzi* cut a piece of the dough the size of a small egg from the flaky pastry portion. Tease this out until it is a thin disc double its original size. Cut a portion of the Swiss roll dough of the same size and pull this out in the same way. Sandwich the two pieces together (the Swiss roll pastry should be uppermost). Spoon the rikotta into the centre and fold the right half over the left to make the traditional *pastizzi* shape with two pointed ends. Place on a lightly oiled baking tray and bake as before.

Qassatat
Small rikotta pies

For the pastry
150 g butter or margarine
400 g plain flour
Pinch of salt
5–6 tbsp cold water
Egg for glaze

For the filling
200 g rikotta
Salt and pepper
3 tbsp parsley, chopped
1 egg, beaten

◆ These maintain a certain popularity despite the fact that they are a poor relation to *pastizzi*. However, they are still good if carefully made.

Make the pastry by rubbing the cold fat into the sieved flour and salt until the mixture resembles fine bread crumbs. Bring it together with water.

Mash the *rikotta* with seasoning, Parmesan and parsley. Stir in the beaten egg.

Roll out the pastry and cut into circles about 9.5 cms in diameter. Place 2 tspn of the filling in the centre of each circle. Do not overfill. Wet the edges of the pastry and gather it up in the shape of a purse or moneybag to cover most of the filling but leaving some showing. Glaze with a little beaten egg.

Place on a lightly oiled baking tray and bake at 200°C/400°F/gas 6 for about 10 minutes. Reduce to 180°C/350°F/gas 4 and bake for a further 15–20 minutes. They should be pale gold in colour. Eat hot or cold.

◆ Make pastry as in the previous recipe. Flaky pastry may be used if preferred. Young, shelled raw broad beans are a typical addition, possibly Gozitan in origin.

Line a wide, shallow, greased pie dish with half the pastry. Beat out the lumps in the *rikotta*, and add seasoning, cheese, parsley and the beaten egg. Stir in the broad beans if they are used. They should be young and tender and their inner skins removed. If using more mature or frozen beans, blanch them in salted water, then skin them before adding to the filling. Spoon the filling into the pastry case. Cover with a lid of pastry or make a trellis pattern with strips. If you have added the broad beans you should use a complete lid and in this case prick it with a fork or make a small hole in the centre and decorate with pastry leaves. In both cases brush with beaten egg. Bake at 200°C/400°F/gas 6 and reduce after the first 15 minutes (as in the previous recipe). The cooking time is approximately 30 minutes. Before placing the pie in the oven, put a baking sheet on the top shelf to heat. This will help cook the bottom of the pie. For those who like *rikotta* sweet, omit beans, parsley and seasoning and dredge the *torta* with sugar.

Torta tal-bajd u l-ġobon

Large rikotta pie

Shortcrust or puff pastry to line and cover a 17.5 cm pie dish
225 g rikotta
Salt and pepper
3 tbsp Parmesan, grated
1 tbsp parsley, chopped
1 egg, beaten
125 g shelled broad beans, inner skins removed (optional)
Egg for glazing

Ravjuletti bl-irkotta

Small fried rikotta pies

For the pastry
200 g plain flour
Pinch of salt
50 g butter
1 egg yolk
2 tbsp cold water

For the filling
225 g rikotta
Salt and pepper
3 tbsp Parmesan, grated
1 tbsp parsley, chopped
1 egg, beaten
Deep oil for frying

◆ This recipe is a variant on the *rikotta*-filled ravioli described on page 130. The difference is that a shortcrust pastry is used, and the resulting parcels are deep fried in oil, not boiled or poached.

Sieve the flour and salt, rub in the fat, add the egg yolk and water to bind. Bring together and rest.

Make the filling as in the previous recipe for small *rikotta* pies. Proceed with the pastry as described in the ravioli recipe. Roll out thinly into an oblong. Cut into strips about 10 cm wide. Place 1 teaspoonful of filling at intervals along one side of each strip. Fold the pastry over the filling and press down to seal it in an envelope. Cut round each mound of *rikotta* in a half-moon shape. Prick lightly once on each side with a fork. Fry in the boiling oil until pale golden and dry on kitchen paper. Serve very hot. An excellent party dish.

Ravjuletti tal-moħħ

Small fried brain pies

1 pig's brain
1 onion, chopped
2 rashers lean, green bacon
25–50 g butter
1 tbsp parsley, chopped
Salt and pepper
Pastry as in the preceding recipe
Deep oil for frying

◆ Our remarks on page 110 about brains in Britain hold good.

Soak the brain in cold salted water and peel off the membranes. Blanch in boiling, salted and vinegared water for 10 minutes. Drain and cool. Cut into neat dice. Cook the onion in the butter (add a little olive oil to prevent burning) with the lid on the pan. Add the finely chopped bacon and cook a few minutes longer. Add the cooked brain cut into pieces. Add parsley and seasoning. Leave to get cold.

Follow the procedure outlined for the small *rikotta*-filled pies, above, in making the pastry and constructing, then frying, the pies.

Barbuljata

Maltese Scrambled eggs

2 or 3 large ripe tomatoes
1 onion, finely chopped
1 tbsp olive oil
25–50 g butter
Chopped garlic to taste
8 eggs
Salt and pepper
1 tbsp parsley or mint, chopped

◆ Peel, deseed and chop the tomatoes. Cook the onion in the oil and a little butter until soft. Add the garlic and the tomatoes. Cook all for a further 5 minutes. Beat the eggs lightly with the salt and pepper and pour them on to the tomatoes and onions, adding the remaining butter and parsley or mint. If you have no fresh herbs, a pinch of the best dried mint may be an adequate substitute. Stir continuously over low heat until the eggs are barely set. Continue to stir once off the heat. Serve with fresh Malta bread, toast or any crusty bread.

Rikotta

◆ The word means 'twice cooked'. The traditional way, remembered by the present generation of great-grandparents, was to use sea water as a curdling agent, like rennet. We do not know whether this is still practised and believe the current method used by Italian manufacturers is to add the whey from cream cheese to full-cream milk. (You could try using the whey from ġbejniet, below.) The ratio of fresh milk to whey is 3:1.

Mix three parts milk to one part whey. Heat together in a bain-marie, stirring frequently, until the temperature reaches 85°C. Stir less often and wait until the temperature reaches 90°C. At this point the mixture should 'break' and stirring should cease while you continue to heat to a maximum of 95°C. Now stir intermittently and very slowly and stop altogether when particles of curd (the *rikotta*) begin to rise to the surface. Turn off the heat and leave in the bain-marie, covered, for about 20 minutes.

Use a slotted spoon to lift the *rikotta* from the whey. Scoop it into a plastic (formerly rush) basket and leave to drain for at least 10 minutes. It is now ready for use and can be kept in the refrigerator for a few days, covered.

Ġbejniet

Small fresh cheeses

1200 ml full cream milk
3–4 tsp good rennet (the strength of different brands varies so we cannot give precise quantities)
two pinches salt
4 small plastic gbejniet *baskets (or authentic rush ones if you can find them)*

◆ *Ġbejniet* are usually made on a small scale on our farms. The industry still thrives and must indeed be growing since, unlike the time when our book was first published, one can buy them in Valletta market and at good delicatessens. Gozo remains less urbanized and is even better served. It is said that the best are made in Żebbuġ (Gozo).

This is a well-tested recipe for those who wish to try. Ideally, unpasteurised fresh milk should be used. Traditionally this should be goats' or sheep's, but cows' milk may be used. Today, most milk needs to be pasteurised.

Heat the milk in a clean heavy saucepan to body temperature (37°C). Stir constantly so the temperature is uniform. Remove from the heat and add rennet and salt. Stir once, then leave for 1 hour, covered with a clean cloth.

Spoon the curd into four baskets which you have placed in a colander, set over a deep dish to catch the whey. You may have some curd left in the pan. This is used to top up the baskets as the whey drains off. After about 6 hours the *ġbejniet* should be fairly set. Turn each cheese over in its basket and refrigerate overnight. The whey is discarded unless you plan to use it for *rikotta*. Eat fresh with sea-salt and pepper and fresh Malta bread. Young broad beans make an excellent accompaniment when they are in season.

Ġbejniet moxxi

Dried ġbejniet

◆ Almost all Gozitan roof tops boast a fairly large meat safe. This is where the cheeses are left to dry to become *ġbejniet moxxi*. These are similar in appearance to the French *crottin de chèvre*. The drying process gives them a delicious nutty flavour. They may be eaten in the usual way or grated in place of Parmesan for sprinkling on spaghetti. When buying *ġbejniet* it is wise to make certain that they are made from pasteurized milk. Undulant fever (also known as Mediterranean or Malta fever), although not as widespread as it used to be, may still be contracted from infected milk (cows', goats' or sheep's).

Ġbejniet tal-bżar

Peppered ġbejniet

◆ Put dried *ġbejniet* in an earthenware jar and sprinkle them very liberally with sea-salt and pepper. Pour over sufficient olive oil, and a little vinegar, to cover them. Cover the jar until ready to eat. Use the vinegar sparingly. You do not want to produce a strong vinegary taste.

Galletti

Hard plain biscuits

15 g fresh yeast or the equivalent in easy-blend or dried yeast (follow the manufacturers' instructions)
150–175 ml warm water
200 g plain flour
Pinch of salt
150 g semolina
25 g butter

◆ Galletti are usually made in two sizes, large and small. The larger ones are the more traditional. When freshly made or bought, they go very well with cheese. Bought *galletti* have deteriorated in quality since our book was first published. Try to make some, just once, even though they are time-consuming. Some members of our family have omitted the yeast from this recipe and claim it made no difference to the result.

Cream the yeast in the water. Sieve the flour and salt into a bowl, add the semolina. Rub in the butter. Add the yeast and enough water until you have a pliable but rather dry dough.

Work a little dough at a time, keeping the rest in the refrigerator to retard the rising. Roll out very thinly on a floured board and cut into rounds using a plain 5 cm cutter. Prick each biscuit with a fork and lay on a floured baking sheet. Bake at 200°C/400°F/gas 6 until just coloured. Cool on a wire tray. When completely cold, store in an airtight tin.

Biskutelli
Rusks

15 g fresh yeast or the equivalent in easy-blend or dried yeast (follow the manufacturers' instructions)
150–175 ml warm water
400 g plain flour
Pinch of salt
50 g butter
1–1½ tsp crushed ainseed
200 g caster sugar

◆ Cream the yeast in the water. Sieve the flour and salt into a bowl, rub in the butter and add the sugar and aniseed. Make a well and add the yeast and water. At least 150 ml water is used, but adjust this quantity to the flour. Bring the mixture together, then turn on to a work surface and knead until you have a pliable, bread-like dough. Return to the bowl and prove in a warm place, covered, until doubled in bulk. This will take longer than bread as the sugar retards the rising.

Return the dough to the work surface; knead briefly to knock it back. Form into 4 elongated cakes and bake on a tray at 200°C/400°F/gas 6 until cooked through, approximately 20 minutes. Allow to cool overnight. Cut each cake into thin slices. Lay out the slices on a tray and bake at 180°C/350°F/gas 4 until crisp and golden, checking frequently that they do not catch. Cool on wire racks.

FROTT U IKEL ĦELU

SWEET THINGS, SYRUPS AND JAMS

Our list of sweet dishes is relatively short, but this does not mean that sugar consumption is low in the Maltese islands. When a sweet course is wanted for a special occasion (family gatherings and celebrations are a regular occurrence) it is customary to order an ornate sweet from a confectioner. This might be a *torta* bursting with ground almonds, or an ice-cream *qassata* filled with candied fruit and roasted nuts.

For every day eating, the main course is followed by fresh fruit. There is nothing more delicious than the purple or pale green figs or the white peaches and perfect plums which abound in the summer months, as well as melons, watermelons, prickly pears and *bambinella* (miniature pears). In winter, oranges are much in demand (and cost accordingly) and our blood oranges are renowned throughout Europe. They gave their name to *Sauce Maltaise*, a recipe believed to originate in the kitchens of the Knights of St John. In a letter written in 1902 by Joseph Chamberlain to Lord Grenfell, Governor of Malta, he thanks him for 'your welcome present of oranges, which are as good as usual and, I am almost inclined to say, the best thing that Malta produces'. A rather dubious compliment.

The traveller Patrick Brydone wrote in 1773: 'The Maltese oranges certainly deserve the character they have of being the finest in the world.

The season continues for upward of seven months; from November until the middle of June during which time those beautiful trees are always covered with abundance of this delicious fruit. Many of them are of the red kind, much superior, in my opinion, to the others, which are rather too luscious. They are produced, I am told, from the common orange-bud engrafted on the pomegranate stock. The juice of this fruit is red as blood, and of a fine flavour. The greatest part of their crop is sent in presents to the different courts of Europe, and to the relations of the chevaliers [i.e. Knights of St John]. It was not without a good deal of difficulty that we procured a few chests for our friends at Naples.

The industry of the Maltese in cultivating their little island is inconceivable. There is not an inch of ground lost in any part of it; and when there was not soil enough, they have brought over ships and boats loaded with it from Sicily, where there is plenty and to spare.'

Brydone would be horrified that, today, not an inch of ground is lost if it can have an apartment block or ostentatious villa built on it. How many ancient orange and other trees have been removed to make way for buildings in some of Malta's most beautiful gardens?

A later traveller, W. I. Monson, reflected on the fame and rarity of the Maltese orange adding, 'the fruit, however, of Malta is delicious; the only thing in such a clime to be dreaded is too much warmth. In the vallies, the fig trees are remarkably fine.'

When Sir Walter Scott visited Malta in 1831, 'he sniffed with great delight the perfume of the new oranges, which hung thickly on each side as [he] drove up the long avenue to the courtyard' of his friend, the diplomatist and poet John Hookham Frère, at San Anton.

The older generation which has lived through one or both world wars strongly believes in the worth of stewed apples several times a week. Certainly some of our apples taste better when they are cooked.

In the recipes which follow, there are few suggestions for cooked fruit. Most are for cakes, biscuits and other combinations of sugar and flour. Many of the sweets we describe are seasonal. *Imbuljuta* and *qagħaq tal-għasel* are prepared at Christmas, when the tangerines which give them both such an exquisite flavour are in season. *Prinjolata* and almond chunks are sold over the islands at Carnival. *Figolli* and *qassatat* are Easter specialities, although *qassatat* now tend to be available all year round. *Kwareżimal* is made during Lent, though it is far too good to be tied up with fasting and abstinence. In early November, to coincide with All Souls, a sweet called *għadam* (bones) is sold. It needs no explanation.

No christening would be complete without *biskuttini tal-lewż morr* and the little *biskuttini tal-magħmudija*, delicately decorated with pale pink and white icing. Sadly, since the first edition of this book, two excellent confectioners have disappeared: Andrea Bonaci in Old Theatre Street Valletta, who sold exquisite cakes with a pale green, crunchy coating (there are some poor imitations about), and the Ġenwiża, in Zejtun, renowned for all their products, particularly *biskuttini tal-lewż morr*.

Fruit

◆ A word about our fruit: in short, another

warning. Many old varieties are in danger of being lost due to European regulations requiring costly registration and patenting, to the concern of producers and conservationists everywhere. In England, the Henry Doubleday Research Association has set up an 'Adopt a Vegetable' scheme to safeguard uncommon varieties of vegetables and fruit for future generations. No doubt Malta is taking heed.

Here, our contribution is to give an idea of the varieties of fruits traditionally grown in Malta. They have some delightful names, often related to those of saints and indicating particular seasons. Some names closely mirror those in other languages (for example French), a sign of introduction to the islands by the Knights of St John (especially true of pears).

Tuffieħ (apples): *Abjad; Aħmar; Pumiċell; ta-Gian-Mattew; ta-Belluga.*

Lanġas (pears): *Bambinella; Settembrina ta-Santa Marija; Fjur t'Awissu; Burutira tal-Vittorja; Anġelika ta-Malta; Dukessa ta-Malta; il Kavalier; Eva Ballet; Madame Ballet; La France; La Kontessa ta-Pariġi; St. Germain; D'Hiver; Cadillac.*

Berquq (apricots): *Berquq Iswed; Berquq ta Mejju; Lixandrina; Damaskina.*

Hawħ (peaches): *Hawħ ta-Malta; Franċiża Bajda; tal-Ponta; ta-Lulju.*

Nuċiprisk (nectarine): *Bajda u Ħamra ta-Malta.*

Larinċ (oranges): *tal-Bakkaljaw; ta-Baħia (ta-Brazil); bizzarrija; tal-għageb ta-San Ġiormu; tad-demm; taż-żokra; fin tawwali; tal-Portugal; ordinarju; qares; zupperit; ta-rjus; tal-Olanda; twil tad-demm; tawwali fin tad-demm; twil tal-*

għafsa; tal-Ġamajka; ta'l Indja (li ifuħ mill ixjed); tal-Kina; tal-qoxra ħoxna; tas-Saliħ (from Gozo).

Pruna (plums): *ta-San Ġwann; Safra Irqieqa; Sewda Ħelwa.*

Ghajn Baqar (cherry plums).

Anzalori (Neapolitan medlar).

Naspli (Japanese medlar).

Omm il-Epp or ***Fomm il-Lipp*** (European medlar).

Ċirasa tal-Malta (Malta cherry): a number of varieties which appear in June and July.

Rummien (pomegranate): *Qares; Bullar; Franċiża; Santa Roża; Demmija; Santa Katerina; San Ġużepp.*

Sfarġel (quince).

Bajtar tax-Xewk (prickly pears): *Isfar ta-Malta; Abjad ta Franża; Aħmar Ingliz.*

Id-Dielja (grapes, literally, the vine): *Barbria; il Belluza; Battuni ta-Gallu; Karminet; Kalabrisa; Katlana; Damaskina; Ġellewża; Gorbina; Grinjola; Insolja; Miġnuna* (literally, mad woman); *Muskatell.*

Ċawsli (white mulberry): *tal-Lombardija; il Bajda; ir-raġel* (literally, the man; in fact this kind does not produce fruit but is grown for its leaves).

Tuta (black mulberry).

Tin (fig): *il parsott; il farkizzan; San Sidori; San Ġwann; bajtar ta-San Ġwann; tal-Buskett; tin ġludi.*

Torta ta l-irkotta ħelwa

Sweet rikotta tart or cheesecake

Shortcrust pastry made with 100–150 g flour
200 g rikotta
2 tbsp glacé cherries, chopped
25 g candied orange peel, chopped

◆ Line a greased 17.5 cm flan tin with pastry. Sieve or mash the *rikotta*, add the other ingredients and spoon into the shell.

Bake at 200°C/400°F/gas 6 for 10 minutes; then reduce to 180°C/350°F/gas 4 for 15–20 minutes, until the pastry is cooked. The *rikotta* will dry out if left longer. Best served cold.

Chopped roasted almonds or hazelnuts and chips of plain chocolate may be added to the *rikotta*. Alternatively, leave out the fruit and nuts and flavour the sweetened *rikotta* with the freshly grated rind of half a lemon. To this you can add a few sultanas. Bake as before.

Mqaret

Date-filled diamonds

For the filling
200 g dates, stoned and chopped
1 tsp grated tangerine zest
1 tsp grated orange zest
Pinch of powdered cloves
1 tbsp anisette liqueur
1 tbsp caster or icing sugar

For the pastry
200 g plain flour
50 g butter
2 tbsp water
Oil for deep frying
Caster sugar for dusting

◆ The word *mqaret* is the plural form of *maqrut*, from the Arabic, meaning lozenge or rhomboid.

Combine the dates and 3 tbsp water in a saucepan. Stir over a low heat for a 4 minutes. Remove from the heat and add all the other filling ingredients. Reserve.

Make the pastry by the rubbing-in method. Some cooks use 1 tbsp orange flower water (*ilma żahar*) and 1 tbsp water as their liquid. Roll out half the pastry at a time into an oblong of 40 × 10 cm. Spoon the filling down one side of the oblong, leaving a small border. Damp the edges and fold over the pastry, pinching well to prevent the filling from running out. Repeat with the rest of the pastry.

Cut these diagonally into 16 diamond-like parallelograms with a sharp knife and rest them in the refrigerator for at least 30 minutes. Fry in deep hot oil until golden. They will darken as they cool. Drain on kitchen paper and sprinkle with caster sugar. It is also possible to bake these on a sheet in a hot oven.

Biskuttini tar-raħal

Village biscuits

4 eggs
350 g caster or golden caster sugar
Grated rind of ½ lemon
Grated rind of ½ orange
3 drops real vanilla essence
Pinch ground caraway or aniseed
500 g self-raising flour

◆ Separate the eggs. Whisk the whites until stiff and whisk in the sugar. Fold in the beaten yolks, orange and lemon rind, vanilla and spices. Some cooks also add a spoonful of apricot or other jam. Sieve the flour and fold it gently but thoroughly into the eggs until you have a pliable dough. Roll into little balls (dust your hands with semolina while you are doing this) and space them generously on a greased and floured baking sheet. Preheat the oven to 200°C/400°F/gas 6 but reduce to 180°C/350°F/gas 4 as soon as the biscuits are inserted. Bake for 20 minutes until a pale cream colour. Cool on racks and store in an airtight tin.

Biskuttini tal-magħmudija

Christening biscuits

8 eggs
700 g caster sugar (for preference, golden and white mixed)
1/2 tsp ground cinnamon
1/2 tsp ground cloves
50 g candied peel, very finely chopped
700 g plain flour
1 tsp baking powder

Royal icing

◆ Known as christening biscuits in Malta, but bride's biscuits (*biskuttini tal-għarusa*) in Gozo. What difference a narrow channel makes.

Separate the eggs and whisk the whites until stiff. Whisk in the yolks. Gradually add the sugar and spices and fold in the peel. Sift the flour and baking powder and fold into the mixture with a palette knife. Do not beat.

Line baking sheets with greaseproof paper, grease lightly with butter or oil and sprinkle with sugar and flour.

Take dessert spoons of the mixture and press between floured hands into rounds or ovals. Space these out well on the baking sheets and bake at 180°C/350°F/gas 4 for 20 minutes until firm. They must not brown. Cool on racks. When quite cold, decorate with curls of white or pink royal icing.

Qagħaq tal-ġulġlien tal-ħmira

Yeasted Sesame Seed Rings

300 g plain flour
15 g fresh yeast
40 g butter
100 g caster sugar
Pinch of ground cloves
½ tsp ground aniseed
Grated rind of 1 orange or tangerine and 1 lemon
Juice of ½ an orange or tangerine, ½ a lemon
Sesame seeds

◆ Prepare a yeast sponge. Sift 200 g of flour into a large basin. Cream the yeast with 125 ml of warm water (25°C), make a well in the flour and add the liquid. Sprinkle over some of the flour from the sides of the basin, cover and leave in a warm place for 60 minutes.

Rub the butter into the remaining 100 g flour. Add the sugar, spices, orange and lemon rind. Mix this with the sponge, adding the citrus juice. Add more warm water if the dough is too dry (but it should not be too slack). Bring the dough together, then turn on to a work surface and knead for 10 minutes. Put to rise, covered, in a warm place for at least I hour, until doubled in bulk.

Return the dough to the work surface and knock out any air bubbles. Divide into 6 or 8 pieces. Roll each piece into a long, even sausage, but more the width of a chipolata. They should not be too thick. Form each into a ring by joining the ends and pressing firmly together. Have a plate well covered with sesame seeds and press each ring down on to the seeds so the top is thickly coated.

Place on greased baking sheet(s), cover again and keep in a warm place until doubled in size. Bake at 200°C/400°F/gas 6 for 25–30 minutes, until golden brown. Cover with a clean tea towel as soon as they come out of the oven and leave until cold. This serves to keep the crust soft.

Qagħaq tal-ġulġlien (ottijiet)

Sesame rings or figures of eight

200 g self-raising flour
100 g caster or icing sugar
75 g butter
Juice and grated rind of 1 lemon and 1 orange
1 egg, beaten
Sesame seeds

◆ Sieve the flour, add the sugar and rub in the butter until the mixture resembles fine bread crumbs. Add the lemon and orange rinds and bind together with the juice and the beaten egg, adding a tiny amount of water. if necessary to make the dough workable.

Break the dough into walnut-sized pieces and roll these into thin sausage shapes. Fashion them into rings as in the preceding recipe. A twist in the middle will convert the circles into figures of eight, which is the traditional shape. Have a quantity of sesame seeds on a plate and press each shape into them so that the top is coated with seed.

Place, well spaced, on a greased baking tray and bake at 200°C/400°F/gas 6, reducing immediately to 180°C/350°F/gas 4, for 20–25 minutes, until golden. You might try reducing the fat content to just 50 g butter for an even crisper texture.

Biskuttini tal-lewż

Almond macaroons

2 egg whites
100 g caster sugar
250 g ground almonds
2 drops almond essence (optional)

◆ Beat the egg whites stiffly. Whisk in the sugar then stir in the ground almonds and the essence, if used. Line baking sheets with foil or greaseproof with a layer of rice paper laid over the top. Drop teaspoonfuls of the mixture well apart on the rice paper and bake at 180°C/350°F/gas 4 for about 10 minutes until pale gold in colour. The macaroons should be soft inside.

Kannoli

Crisp rikotta pastries

For the pastry
200 g plain flour
3 tsp caster or icing sugar
1–2 tsp sieved cocoa powder
4 tsp butter
2 tbsp Marsala or red wine
125 ml cold water

For the filling
400 g rikotta
50 g bitter chocolate
100 g candied orange and citron peel or glacé cherries
50 g icing sugar
100 g blanched, roasted almonds or hazel nuts

Oil for deep frying
Lemon rind for the fat

◆ *Kannoli* are perhaps best bought from a professional confectioner. Look for one who fills them at the time of purchase so the pastry remains crisp. Here is a recipe for you to try, but first you must buy the special metal tubes for moulding the *kannoli*, from Balbi in Merchants Street, Valletta or Cathedral Street, Sliema, or Albion Stores in Merchants Street.

Make the pastry. Knead lightly until it feels elastic. If you knead too vigorously, large air bubbles will form in the frying, causing the pastry shells to part at the join. Rest it in a cool place while you prepare the filling. Mash the rikotta; chop the chocolate, cherries or citrus peel, and the nuts; mix everything together.

Roll the pastry out very thinly. Cut into rounds the size of a saucer and place each one round one of the metal tubes, pressing the join firmly. Heat the oil and drop in a piece or two of lemon rind. Fry the *kannoli* a few at a time, turning them over until they are evenly brown. Do not let them get too dark. Replace the lemon rind when it gets brown. Drain on kitchen paper and leave to cool.

Where deep-fat frying is rarely practised in a household, the Chinese wok (provided it is flat-bottomed) is an excellent pan to use. It uses less oil, and is more manageable than the straight-sided pan used in most European kitchens.

Fill the pastries just before serving, using a teaspoon or piping bag. Each end may be studded with a piece of candied peel or dipped into more chopped nuts.

Torta tal-marmurat
Almond and chocolate pie

For the pastry
200 g flour
2 level tbsp caster sugar
100 g butter
1 egg yolk

For the filling
200 g almonds
200 g candied orange peel
75–100 g bitter chocolate
100 g caster sugar
3 eggs, beaten
1 scant tsp cinnamon

50 g bitter chocolate to finish

◆ Sieve the flour, and add the sugar. Rub in the butter until the mixture resembles fine bread crumbs. Add the egg yolk and 1–2 tbsp cold water to bind. Mix well with your finger tips, kneading lightly until you have a pliable dough. Chill in the refrigerator for a short time. Roll to fit a greased, shallow 17.5 cm pie dish, allowing an overhang of 2.5 cm.

Blanch the almonds; chop them finely or grind them coarsely. They should not be as fine as shop-bought ground almonds. Chop the candied peel. Combine the nuts, peel and sugar in a bowl. Grate in the chocolate. How much will depend on your taste for chocolate, but it should not overpower the almonds. Add cinnamon and eggs. Spoon this mixture into the pastry case. Turn the overhang of the pastry over towards the centre of the pie, giving a 2.5 cm border.

Bake at 200°C/400°F/gas 6 for 15 minutes, then reduce to 160°C/325°F/gas 3 and continue until the pastry is pale golden.

Melt 50 g chocolate in a bain-marie and pour it over the still warm pie. Leave to cool. Home-candied peel is far preferable to that bought from shops. The recipe which follows was given us by one of our aunts.

Kunfettura
Candied Peel

8 or 9 oranges or tangerines
1 tsp salt
400 g sugar

◆ Take only fruit in good condition, preferably untreated and organically grown. Peel and cut each whole peel into 6 or 8 pieces. Place in a bowl and cover with salted water. Leave for 2 or 3 days. Drain and rinse.

Cover with fresh water in a saucepan. Simmer until the peel feels tender. Drain again and reserve peel in a clean bowl.

Dissolve the sugar in 250 ml of water over

low heat – do not stir, but shake the pan from time to time – then bring to a boil and simmer for 10 minutes. Pour over the peel, cover and stand in a cool place for approximately 4 days.

Pour off the syrup into a saucepan and bring to the boil. Add the peel and let it boil until the syrup is clear and almost all absorbed by the peel. Turn into a lightly buttered tin or dish. Sprinkle with a little more sugar and leave to dry and candy. Store in an airtight jar when cold and use as needed.

Xkunvat

Crisp pastry ribbons

200 g plain flour with ½ tsp baking powder
25 g butter
1 egg yolk
2 tsp sugar
3 tbsp orange flower water and/ or brandy
Malta honey, coloured sugar or hundreds and thousands

◆ This pastry sweet is served on festive occasions, especially first birthdays. A child's first birthday is also marked by the *quċċija* ceremony. A tray is presented to the infant, filled with a variety of objects. The first thing that he (or she) picks is augury of a future vocation. Odds were shortened by offering girls eggs, needles, or other symbols of reproduction and domesticity, while boys got books, thermometers and so forth. Would-be nuns (the parents would have decided) were offered rosaries.

Sieve the flour into a bowl and add the sugar. Rub in the butter until the mixture resembles fine bread crumbs. Bind with the egg yolk, the orange flower water or brandy, adding a tiny amount of water only if necessary. Roll the pastry out thinly and cut with a pastry wheel into strips approximately 1.25 cm wide and 13 cm long. Fry a few strips at a time, rolling each strip up tightly along its length just before dropping into hot oil. The roll will unfurl, giving a spiral. Fry until golden. Drain well on kitchen paper, and cool.

Pile on a glass dish and trickle over good

Malta honey. Decorate with coloured sugar or hundreds and thousands. Coloured sugar is traditional, the other is a substitute probably adopted after the Second World War.

Coloured sugar is made thus. Take a teaspoon of sugar and put it in a teacup. Put the tip of a skewer into a bottle of food colouring, then use it to stir the sugar. In this way you will not overdo the amount of colouring. The usual practice is to have two colours (red and green) and white. The brazen cheerfulness of the decoration is authentic.

Kwareżimal

Lenten almond cakes

200 g blanched almonds
200 g plain flour, sifted
250 g caster or golden caster sugar
1 scant tsp cinnamon
Orange flower water
Grated rind of 1 lemon, 1 orange and 1 tangerine
Malta honey and pistachio nuts or additional almonds

◆ This is made during Lent and contains no fat or eggs, although the Lenten fast is no longer adhered to. The word *kwareżimal* refers to *quaresima*, literally the quadragesima, the forty days of Lent.

Lightly toast or roast the almonds. Grind coarsely. Mix with the flour, sugar, cinnamon, rinds and a little orange-flower water. Add just enough water to make a stiff dough. Knead lightly until well amalgamated and shape into ovals, approximately 17.5 cm long, 5 cm wide and 2 cm thick. Place on greased and floured baking trays and bake at 190°C/375°F/gas 5 for about 20 minutes.

While still hot, spread with Malta honey and press on chopped, unsalted pistachio nuts or chopped roasted almonds or hazel nuts. The only honey which resembles the exquisite Malta honey is Greek Hymettus, from the mountain of that name. It is now extremely difficult to obtain the real Malta honey (which is flavoured with wild thyme) despite what the label (and the vendors) say.

Figolli

Easter characters

For the pastry
350 g caster sugar
800 g plain flour, sifted
400 g butter
Grated rind of 1 lemon
4 egg yolks, beaten

For the almond paste
600 g caster or icing sugar
2–3 egg whites
Grated rind of 1 lemon
A few drops orange flower water
600 g almonds, ground

To finish
Glacé icing
Royal icing
Small Easter eggs

◆ *Figolli* are almond pastries cut out to represent symbolic figures. They come into their own at Easter time. It is wisest to buy them from a reputable confectioner. Some charities make and sell them too, but beware of the quality, no matter how deserving the charity.

You will need the metal cutters. If you cannot obtain these, you can make your own templates, like gingerbread men, out of cardboard. The traditional shapes are men, women, fish and baskets, the last perhaps being fertility symbols. More recently, new shapes have begun to emerge, such as butterflies, lambs and cars. A shop window filled with these figolli is a colourful sight. The human shapes are easily identifiable by the old-fashioned oleograph faces stuck on to the icing. An Easter egg wrapped in coloured paper is an essential part of the decoration.

Make the pastry by mixing the sugar with the flour, then rubbing in the butter until the mixture resembles fine crumbs. Add the grated lemon rind and the yolks, mixed with a little water to make a pliable dough. Leave to chill.

Add the sugar, orange flower water and lemon rind to the ground almonds, and bind with the egg whites.

Roll out the pastry and cut out your shapes. Make two of each figure as they will be sandwiched with almond paste. Lay the first shape on a greased and floured baking tray, spread with almond paste, leaving a small margin. Lay the second shape over the top and press the edges together. It helps if you wet the edges with a pastry brush to ensure adhesion. Bake at 200°C/400°F/gas 6 for 5 minutes, then at

180°C/350°F/gas 4, for about 20 minutes, until pale golden. Cool on the tray.

When cold, coat with glacé icing, then decorate with royal icing in a different colour, but nothing too gaudy. While the icing is soft, press a small, foil-wrapped Easter egg in the middle of each shape. As children we used to be intrigued by the egg right in the middle of the man or woman's tummy. Ground almonds are very expensive and full-size *figolli* are enormous. You might like to consider making half the quantity of this recipe and making the *figolli* half the size, using tiny sugar-coated eggs. Less traditional but still good.

Pasta rjali

Marzipan sweets

400 g caster sugar
5 tbsp orange juice
400 g ground almonds
2–3 drops genuine almond essence
Food colouring, colours according to representations worked, but they should be pale or pastel

◆ Dissolve the sugar in the orange juice over a low heat. Bring to a boil, without stirring but shake the pan from time to time. Simmer for about 30 minutes. Allow to get almost cold before adding the ground almonds, the essence and the food colouring. When quite cold, form into shapes and roll in icing sugar.

This mixture can be used to stuff dates. Shapes can be what you will, although different coloured fruit, with cloves for stalks, are popular, especially at Christmas. Place in little paper cases.

Qagħaq tal-għasel
Treacle rings

For the filling
800 g tin treacle or golden syrup
An equal volume of water (use the tin to measure)
200 g sugar
Grated rind of a tangerine, a lemon and an orange
1 tbsp candied peel, chopped
Pinch of ground cloves
2 tbsp apricot jam
350 g semolina

For the pastry
750g plain flour
30 g butter
2 egg yolks

◆ These can be found all the year round but are particularly associated with Christmas. There is even a traditional carol that celebrates their making.

The filling is made the day before it is needed. Place all the ingredients, except the semolina, in a large saucepan. Slowly bring to a boil and begin to add the semolina a little at a time, stirring carefully and constantly. Cook for a few more minutes after the mixture has come to a boil, so that it is thick. Cover when cold and refrigerate for 12 hours.

Make the pastry by sieving the flour, and rubbing in the butter until the mixture resembles bread crumbs. Add the beaten egg yolks and cold water to bind. The pastry will keep in the refrigerator for some days.

Divide the pastry into six pieces and roll out one piece at a time. Cut each piece into individual rectangles approximately 10 cm wide and 17.5 cm long. Take a generous dessertspoonful of the filling and shape into a sausage as thick as an outsize finger and as long as the pastry rectangle. This can be a sticky process. It helps if the work surface is well dusted with semolina Place the filling in the centre of the pastry rectangle and fold over to cover. There is no need to damp the edges. Make into a ring by bringing the two ends together. Repeat the process until you have used up all the pastry and filling ingredients.

Dust the baking sheet with semolina and place the rings on the trays. Take a sharp knife or razor and slash each pastry in 6 different places then lift the openings to let the filling show through. Bake at 190°C/375°F/gas 5 until the pastry is barely coloured. The almost white pastry makes a striking contrast with the dark pockets of the treacle filling. This recipe makes a very large amount, but the *qagħaq* can be stored and eaten a few at a time.

Qagħqa tal-kavatelli
Rich treacle ring

For the pastry
240 g butter
550 g plain flour, sifted
200 g caster sugar
2 drops of genuine almond essence
50 ml anisette liqueur
Juice of 1 lemon, 1 orange and 1 tangerine
Oil for deep frying

For the sauce
550 g blanched almonds
800 g tin treacle
3 tbsp caster sugar
Grated rind of 6 tangerines
Grated rind of 3 oranges and 3 lemons
Coloured granulated sugar to decorate

◆ We believe this is a traditional recipe, rarely encountered anywhere. *Kavatelli* is a regional Italian term for dumplings, and this dish resembles a pile of dumplings, albeit sweet.

Make the pastry by rubbing the butter into the flour and sugar. Add the almond essence. Bind it with the anisette and fruit juices. Use the minimum amount of liquid to bind. Break off pieces of pastry. Roll lightly into thin sausage shapes and cue these into pieces the size of a small walnut. Deep fry in fresh hot oil then drain on kitchen paper.

Roast the blanched almonds lightly. Chop finely. Put the treacle, sugar and grated rinds in a large saucepan and heat slowly until the sugar dissolves. Continue cooking and stirring for about 10 minutes. Gently fold in the chopped almonds and the cold pastry balls.

Arrange the mixture into a ring shape on a large china dish. Colour the sugar in the way described in the *xkunvat* recipe, above. Have three colours: red, green and white. Scatter them all over. Hundreds and thousands are a post-war innovation.

Eat small quantities of dishes like this unless you want to ruin your skin, teeth and figure. We wonder about the treacle used in this and the preceding dishes. It seems likely it was a Victorian colonial substitute for honey.

Soufflé

Maltese trifle

375 ml home-made egg custard (some of it may be chocolate flavoured)
6 large slices of sponge cake
2–3 tbsp apricot or strawberry jam
125 ml brandy, sherry or rum
300 g rikotta
3 tbsp caster sugar
50 g dark chocolate, chopped
50 g candied peel, chopped

To finish
2 egg whites
50 g caster sugar
Bitter chocolate, chopped
Almonds, roasted, chopped

◆ This bears no resemblance to French hot or cold soufflés and we have no idea how it acquired the name.

Use a large glass bowl. Pour in a layer of custard. Slice the sponge cake and spread with jam. Arrange a layer over the custard. Sprinkle with brandy, sherry or rum. Beat the lumps out of the *rikotta* and mix with the caster sugar, chocolate and candied peel. Lay a layer of this on the sponge cake. Repeat the process, continuing until the ingredients have been used up. Finish with a layer of custard.

Whisk the egg whites until stiff. Whisk in the caster sugar. Spoon over the trifle, decorating with more chopped chocolate and some chopped roasted almonds. Clearly the meringue topping must have evolved in the absence of cream.

Imbuljuta

Hot chestnut 'soup'

400–500 g good quality dried chestnuts (in Malta these are known as qastan tal imbuljuta)
1 heaped tbsp cocoa powder
150 g caster sugar
A large piece of tangerine peel cut into thin strips or finely chopped

◆ This is a winter dish, traditional for early on Christmas morning, after midnight mass.

Wash the chestnuts and discard any faulty ones (which is why we have given the extra amount in the ingredients). Place in a large bowl with water to cover and leave to soak overnight. The next day, remove any loose pieces of skin. Cook the chestnuts in the soaking water, until tender. (You will save time if you use a pressure cooker.) Add the other ingredients and continue cooking for about half an hour. It should be thickish in 30 minutes, but may need longer. Adjust sugar or cocoa to taste. Serve hot in soup bowls. A contemporary addition might be whipped fresh cream.

Prinjolata
Pine nut cake

Approximately 24 sponge fingers (boudoir biscuits) or biskuttini tar-raħal
100 g unsalted butter
2 tsp icing sugar
1 tbsp pine nuts or blanched almonds, chopped

2 portions American frosting, each made separately and using:
200g caster sugar
Pinch cream of tartar
1 egg white, beaten
2 drops vanilla essence

For the decoration
50g pine nuts
10 glacé cherries
25 g bitter chocolate, melted

◆ This decorative pudding belongs so the hectic days of carnival. The name comes from the Italian *pignoli* (pine nuts). Of late, the quality of confectioners' *prinjolata* has decreased alarmingly, though prices have risen. Decorations are garish, using cheap cherries and no pine nuts, and it has gelatinous white icing when it should be dry and brittle.

Grease a pudding basin or cake tin. Break each sponge finger in half. Soften the butter and beat to a cream. Add the icing sugar and beat until creamy and pale. Set aside.

For the first portion of American frosting dissolve the sugar in 75 ml water over a low heat. Shake the pan from time to time. Add the cream of tartar (dissolved in 1 tsp water), cover and bring to a boil. Remove the lid and boil the syrup steadily to 116°C (soft ball). Stop from cooking any further by plunging the base of the pan in cold water, then pour the hot syrup in a steady stream into the egg white, whisking all the while until it holds a peak. Add vanilla essence.

Stir in the reserved butter cream immediately. Add the chopped almonds. Coat each sponge finger with this mixture. Assemble them in the basin in concentric layers cemented by the cream filling. Smooth the top, cover and refrigerate overnight. Turn on to a serving dish.

Make a second portion of frosting; without extra butter cream. When ready, coat the entire *prinjolata*. Stud with pine nuts and cherries, then pour over melted chocolate in thin threads. For a less lurid appearance, use only pine nuts, with a few skinned pistachios.

Ħobż tal-anġli
Angels' bread

4 slices of day-old bread
Jam
125 ml milk
1 egg, beaten
Butter and sunflower oil
Caster sugar
Cinnamon, powdered

◆ Sandwich the slices of bread with jam, removing the crusts if you prefer. Cut each sandwich in half. Pour the milk into a deep plate and dip the bread so that it absorbs the milk. Leave covered for 1 hour. Dip the sandwiches in beaten egg, then fry on both sides in hot oil and butter until golden. Serve hot, sprinkling with caster sugar and cinnamon.

Żeppoli or *sfineċ ta-San Ġużepp*
St Joseph's fritters

125 g strong flour
1 tsp caster sugar
100 g butter
3 medium eggs, beaten
Oil for deep frying

Rikotta *filling as for* kannoli, *page 172*
Malta honey
Roasted almonds or hazelnuts, chopped

◆ The name, of course, comes from Guzeppi and these are sold on St. Joseph's feast day, March 19th. The older generation will remember that some of the best *żeppoli* used to be sold by a confectioner named Amabile Mifsud, known affectionately as Mabbli, whose shop was in Dingli Circus, Sliema.

Sift the flour and sugar on to greaseproof paper. Melt the butter in 250 ml water in a heavy pan. Bring to the boil and immediately tip in all the flour. Beat vigorously until the mixture comes away from the sides of the pan. Cool slightly. Add the eggs, a little at a time, beating very thoroughly for about 10 minutes, until you have a smooth, glossy paste. The mixture must not be too runny, keep back some of the egg if this appears a risk.

The traditional recipe is for deep frying, though *żeppoli* can also be baked. To deep fry, drop heaped teaspoons of the mixture into fresh boiling oil. Lift when golden and drain on kitchen paper. Otherwise, preheat the oven to 200°C/400°F/gas 6. Grease a baking sheet then run it under cold water. This creates steam which helps the choux pastry to rise. Place heaped teaspoons well apart on the baking sheet. Place in the oven and after about 5 minutes increase the temperature to 220°C/225°F/gas 7 and cook for a further 10 minutes until risen and golden. Cool on a rack.

Slit the pastry shells with a knife immediately and remove any uncooked, moist mixture from inside. When cold, fill with the same *rikotta* mixture prepared for *kannoli* on page 194, above. Arrange on an attractive dish and trickle best Malta honey over them. Sprinkle with chopped, roasted almonds or hazelnuts.

Il 'cake' ta-Pawla Vella

Pawla Vella's cake

◆ Pawla Vella worked in our grandmother's family for more than 50 years. This is her recipe. Marsala gives the cake its special flavour. Use one of good quality from Sicily. It is also important to use the correct size cake tin with a diameter of 17.5 cm.

125 g softened butter
150 g caster sugar
3 eggs
75 g mixed candied peel. chopped
75 g sultanas
75 g raisins
175 g plain flour sifted with 1 tsp baking powder
4 tbsp Marsala

Grease the tin and line with greaseproof or silicone paper. Cream the butter thoroughly. Pawla herself would have used a wooden spoon and lots of energy. Add the caster sugar a little at a time, and beat until it is white, soft and creamy. Add the eggs, one at a time, beating well after each addition. Fold in the fruit, mixed with 2 tbsp of the flour. Use a palette knife to fold in the remaining flour and baking powder. Substitute 1 tbsp of cornflour for the same amount of flour for a lighter and softer cake. Do not beat any more. Add enough Marsala to give a dropping consistency. Bake at 180°C/350°F/gas 4, in the centre of the oven, for approximately 1 hour, until a skewer or knife point comes out clean. Turn out and cool. You could substitute chopped dates and almonds or walnuts for some or all of the fruit.

Pastizzotti tal-qastan
Chestnut tartlets

600 g fresh chestnuts
1 tbsp good marmalade
50 g bitter chocolate, melted
Grated rind of 1 lemon and 1 orange or tangerine
1 tsp sugar
2–3 tsp rum

Shortcrust pastry (made with 300 g flour)
Beaten egg for glazing

◆ Peel the chestnuts; simmer until they are soft. Grind them in a food processor or pass through a food mill. Moisten, if necessary, with a little water, but the final purée should be dry. Add the other filling ingredients. Taste and adjust for sweetness. Leave to cool.

Roll the pastry and line 12 greased tartlet tins. Fill with the chestnut mixture. Either lay a cross of two pastry strips, or cover each tartlet with a pastry lid, in which you cut a cross with scissors through which the filling will show. Glaze with beaten egg (or just egg white). Bake at 200°C/400°F/gas 6 for 15–20 minutes.

French tinned chestnut purée is a very acceptable substitute. However, if sweetened purée is used, omit any extra sugar and moderate the amount of marmalade. Indeed, add more fresh citrus rind.

Budina tal-biskuttelli
Rusk pudding

8 large rusks
500 ml milk
4 eggs, beaten
4 tbsp caster sugar
2–3 tbsp raisins or sultanas or chopped dates
Grated rind of ½ lemon and ½ orange or tangerine
Pinch of mixed spice or just a grating of nutmeg

◆ In Malta and Gozo rusks are sold by all bakers and grocers. Common throughout the Mediterranean, in Greece they are known as *paximadhi* and are often fed to dogs, who appreciate them very much.

Break the rusks into bite-sized pieces and soak them in enough milk to cover. Leave 12 hours. Stir with a fork to remove any lumps. Add the eggs, sugar, fruit, grated rinds and spice. Add any milk that remains and taste for sweetness. Butter an appropriate pie dish, allowing room for the pudding to rise, and pour in the mixture. Bake at 160°C/325°F/gas 3 for 45–60 minutes, until set. Serve warm or cold. Brandy, whisky or Marsala may be substituted for some of the milk.

Krustini
Hard spice biscuits

400 g plain flour
150 g caster sugar
100 g butter
100 ml sunflower or groundnut oil
Grated rind of 1 lemon
50 g unblanched almonds, chopped
25 g finely chopped candied peel
Pinch of mixed spice
1 egg, beaten
2 tsp lemon juice

◆ Sieve the flour into a basin, add the sugar and rub in the butter and oil until the mixture resembles fine bread crumbs. Add the grated rind, chopped almonds, peel and spice. Mix in the egg and lemon juice to form a dough; add a little water if it does not quite hold together.

Cut into four portions and shape each into a long roll. Place on a greased baking sheet and mark with a knife (but not all the way through) into slices the width of a biscuit. Bake at 180°C/350°F/gas 4 for 20–25 minutes. Remove from the oven and cool for a few minutes. Slice into individual biscuits and return to the oven for a few more minutes. Remove when they begin to turn brown. Cool on a rack and store in an airtight tin.

Qubbajt
Maltese nougat

800 g caster sugar
300 g roasted almonds or hazelnuts, or lightly roasted sesame seeds
1 tsp freshly powdered cinnamon

◆ *Qubbajt* is sold at every *festa*, as well as by confectioners throughout the year. At the *festa*, a pair of ornate scales forms the centrepiece on the high nougat-seller's stall. We give a recipe for the clear, golden toffee nougat, not the creamy white variety.

Oil a shallow baking tray and line first with greaseproof then a sheet of rice paper

Dissolve the sugar in 250 ml water over low heat in a heavy saucepan, shaking but not stirring. Boil to 154°C (crack).

Lightly grease a marble or other slab with a little oil mixed with water and spread the nuts or sesame seeds over it. Sprinkle the cinnamon, then pour the hot syrup over. Turn and work the mixture with two spatulas. When it starts to harden, spoon it into the rice paper case and leave to cool. Remove the greaseproof and leave the edible rice paper.

Ġelat tat-tut

Mulberry ice-cream

300 ml single cream
5 egg yolks, beaten
125 g caster or icing sugar
2 drops vanilla essence
500 g mulberries
300 ml double cream
Lemon juice (optional)

◆ At the end of the War, we had lived for so long on baked beans and the delights of the Victory Kitchens (indebted and thankful though we were to them) that much joy was experienced when food began to be imported again. One item which few people would want to buy today was tinned cream but at the time we thought it wonderful. Victor, our father, used it to make this ice-cream. The mulberries were a gift, dark and juicy, resting on their shiny dark green leaves. The metallic flavour of the cream would be counteracted by quantities of lemon juice. The recipe can be adapted for other fruits and flavours.

Heat the single cream carefully, until almost boiling. Do not allow to boil. Pour on to the egg yolks and beat thoroughly. Stir in the sugar and heat in a bain-marie until a thick custard is formed. Add vanilla essence and allow to get almost cold. Liquidize and sieve the fruit. Whip the double cream until thick. Fold the fruit and cream into the custard. Adjust the taste with lemon juice and sugar. Freeze or churn in your accustomed way.

Mulberry Water Ice and Sorbet

300–600 ml water
250 g caster sugar
Juice of 1 lemon
Juice of 1 orange or tangerine
500 g mulberries
3–5 tbsp kirsch
2 egg whites (for sorbet)

◆ Dissolve the sugar in 300 ml water over low heat. Simmer for 5 minutes. Cool. Add citrus juices. Liquidize and sieve the mulberries. Add to the syrup. Add the kirsch. Freeze or churn according to your accustomed method.

For a sorbet, freeze the water ice quite hard. Beat the egg whites until stiff but not dry. Add spoonfuls of the mulberry ice one by one. The mixture will grow into a velvety mass. As soon as it is all incorporated, re-freeze until it is firm. Serve in little cups or glasses.

Ġulebb tal-ħarrub
Carob syrup

800 g carobs or locust beans
800 g sugar
Half tsp cloves, ground
Whisky (optional)

◆ This is a delicious syrup, which used to be popular in winter and thought an excellent cough remedy. It is said that St. John the Baptist was kept alive by carobs during his 40 days in the wilderness. Sweet carob lozenges can sometimes be bought at the entrance to Valletta. The Latin name for Carob is *Ceratonia Siliqua*.

Wipe the pods dean with a cloth, wash in 2 or 3 changes of water if very dirty. Allow to dry a little. Roast on a wide baking sheet at 190°C/375°F/gas 5 for about 10 minutes, in one layer. Cool, then break each pod into 3 pieces. Soak overnight in 1.5 litres water. Bring to the boil in the same water; simmer for 30 minutes. Drain the liquid into another pan, pressing the pods to extract all the juice. Discard the pods.

Add the sugar and cloves to the juices. Allow the sugar to dissolve over low heat then boil steadily for 30 minutes. Cool completely, add whisky to taste. (The quantity of cloves is also variable to taste.) Pour into sterilized bottles or jars and seal immediately. More water may be added if the mixture is too thick.

Cyprus produces a Ġulebb (called Teratsomelo or Pekmez) with no added sugar. It is equally rich and syrupy and quite sweet enough. If you have a carob tree in your garden you might like to experiment with Ġulebb but omitting the sugar. The Cypriots also produce carob sweets similar to our own – they are known as Pastelli. Carob products are also recommended for constipation.

Kunserva tal-isfarġel
Quince jam

1 kg quinces
1 kg sugar
2–3 lemons
300 ml water
A few drops of real vanilla essence

◆ Wipe, peel and core the quinces; cut the fruit into small dice or grate. Soak in a bowl with the water and the juice and sliced shell of 1 lemon for 60 minutes.

Remove the lemon slices and pour the quinces and water into a preserving pan. Simmer for 30 minutes. Add the sugar. Dissolve slowly over a low heat, then boil for 15 minutes. Add the juice from the other lemons. Boil to 105°C (set) or test on a saucer for setting. If ready, take off the heat, stir for a few minutes, then leave until a skin begins to form. Pot in sterilized, heated jars, as above.

Kunserva tal-bergamott
Bergamot jam

700 g raw peel of bergamots

To finish
850g white sugar
250 ml water
Salt

◆ The bergamot is the most fragrant of all citrus and the peel is used, especially in France, for sweet making: candied and dipped in dark chocolate, and in the famous *bergamottes de Nancy*. It is also used in scents: read Patrick Süskind's vivid novel *Perfume* for a description.

Peel the fruit and weigh the rind. The weight will establish how much sugar and water will be needed to agree with the proportions given in the list of ingredients. Cover the peel with water, with 2 tsp salt. Soak for 4 days, changing the water once. Drain.

Boil the rinds in fresh unsalted water until tender. Drain. Mince the rind or slice it according to whether you prefer it coarse or fine.

Put the sugar, water and peel in a preserving pan. Dissolve the sugar over a low heat, stirring occasionally. Boil to setting point, 105°C, or test on a saucer for set. Stir for 5 minutes to mix in the scum, which need not be removed. Leave for 10 minutes to ensure the peel is distributed. Pot up the jam in sterilised, heated jars and seal immediately.

Kunserva tad-tadam
Tomato Jam

1200 g tomatoes
Sugar
6 cloves
2 bay leaves
A piece of lemon zest

◆ Choose ripe but not soft tomatoes, preferably the flat variety (*tadam ċatt*). Peel and deseed, but press the seeds through a sieve and retain all their juices. They help to set the jam.

Weigh the tomato pulp and add an equal quantity of sugar. Join these to the strained juices in a preserving pan. Do not overfill the pan as this particular jam rises more than any other in the boiling. Add cloves, bay leaves and lemon rind. Dissolve the sugar over a low heat, stirring occasionally. Boil to setting point, 105°C. Test for set, then stir for 5 minutes to mix in the scum, which need not be removed. Leave undisturbed for a further 5 minutes. Lift out the bay leaves and lemon rind. Pot in sterilised, heated jars and seal immediately. This quantity will produce just 3 or 4 jars of really exquisite jam.

Kunserva tal-larinġ tal-bakkaljaw
Marmalade

1.75 kg Seville oranges
2 lemons
½ grapefruit
3 kg sugar

◆ We make no apologies for including a recipe for that supposedly quintessential English conserve. We do so because there are so many orange trees in the Maltese islands but not everyone has a good recipe. Many people are disappointed with their results, others just leave the fruit to rot on the tree because they don't know how to use them. We are uncertain of the origin of the word *bakkaljaw* for Seville orange, since this means salt cod in Maltese and other European languages.

Marmalade derives from the Portugese word *marmelo* (quince), but modern marmalade is a British creation. The Scots established it as a breakfast food and it spread through the Victorian empire. However, it was the Arabs who brought lemon and orange trees to southern Europe, as well as the irrigation methods which enabled them to survive the hot dry summers. They also introduced sugar cane and exported both sugar and bitter oranges to northern Europe during the Middle Ages.

Wash all the fruit, pierce each one with a skewer in 3 or 4 places and simmer in 4000 ml water in a large covered saucepan until soft, about 2 hours. Remove fruit and reserve all the liquid. Either reduce it by boiling, or add more water, until you have half the original quantity (i.e. 2000 ml). Grease a preserving pan with a little butter and add the liquid.

Cut the fruit in half. Remove the pips and tie them in a muslin bag. Attach this with a piece of string to the handle of the preserving pan. Remove the pulp and add it to the pan. Slice or chop the peel coarsely and add that to the pan. Bring to boiling point, add the sugar and simmer until dissolved. Briskly boil to reach 105°C, pressing the muslin bag of pips at intervals against the side of the pan to release the pectin. Test for set. Turn off the heat and stir for 5 minutes to mix in the scum, which need not be removed. Leave for 10 minutes to ensure the fruit is distributed. Pot up in sterilized, heated jars and seal immediately.

Oranges may be frozen (unwashed, straight after picking or buying) and used several months later. Let them thaw before proceeding.

Kunserva tal-mandolin

Tangerine marmalade

3 large lemons
Tangerines to make the weight up to 1250 g
3000 ml water
1100 g sugar
Large pinch of tartaric acid

◆ The process is the same as for the orange marmalade above, except that the tangerines will soften in about 40 minutes and only the lemons will need to cook for longer. Tartaric acid is added during the final boiling to make the marmalade look clearer. Since the pith is nor removed, there is a tendency for it to be cloudy.

ZALEZ

SAUCES

We give here the recipes for sauces mentioned earlier in the book and a few additional ones from *Ctieb tal Chcina* (already mentioned) because we found them new and intriguing. We have decided to include the two non-Maltese sauces (Mayonnaise and Bechamel) on the grounds that they have international status and also because we would like to encourage people to make them at home rather than to buy them in packets and jars. Not surprisingly we begin with Tomato Sauces since they are the ones most used in Mediterranean countries. Sundried tomatoes became one of the most popular discoveries amongst cookery writers of the 1980s and 90s. We remember the beautiful sight of tomatoes drying on dishes and plates in the hot sun of our parents' garden when we were very small children, though we can't remember how long the process took. What stands out in the memory is the glistening sea salt sprinkled on them and the powerful earthy smell. The resulting tomato puree can, of course, be used for tomato sauce if fresh or tinned tomatoes are not available, as well as being an invaluable addition to many other sauces and dishes.

Zalza tad-tadam frisk

Fresh tomato sauce (1)

*800 g fresh tomatoes (*ċatti *or* żenguli*)*
2 tbsp olive oil
1 onion, finely chopped
3 cloves garlic, chopped
1 bay leaf
Salt and pepper
1 tsp sugar

1 stick celery, chopped (optional)
Marjoram, mint or oregano, chopped (optional)
Double cream (optional)

◆ Fresh tomato sauce should be made when tomatoes are at their best and are both plentiful and cheap. At other times, tinned peeled tomatoes may be used.

Wash the tomatoes and halve them. Place them in a saucepan with water to cover. Bring to a boil and simmer gently until tender. Blend, skins and all, in a liquidizer or processor, then sieve the resulting purée. Reserve.

Heat the oil and cook the chopped onion until just beginning to take colour. Add the garlic, bay leaf and seasoning. Add the tomato. Simmer until thick – about 30 minutes. Taste for seasoning, adjusting with sugar if necessary.

A finely chopped stick of celery and some chopped fresh marjoram, mint or oregano may be added to the sauce while it is simmering. Some cooks add a little cream just before serving.

Fresh tomato sauce (2)

*800 g fresh tomatoes (*ċatti *or* żenguli)
1 onion, finely chopped
2 tbsp olive oil
3 cloves of garlic, chopped
1 bay leaf
Salt and pepper
1 tsp sugar
25 g butter
2 tbsp basil, torn

◆ Wash and peel the tomatoes. Remove the seeds. Soften the onion in the oil, add the garlic, tomatoes and seasoning. Simmer until well reduced. Adjust the seasoning, if necessary with sugar. Just before serving, stir the butter into the sauce and add the basil leaves.

Fresh tomato sauce (3)

*600 g tomatoes (*ċatti *or* żenguli)
3 cloves garlic, finely chopped
100 g fresh basil leaves, chopped
Knifepoint of hot red chilli, chopped
4 tbsp olive oil
Salt and pepper

◆ This should only be made when you can get fruit of the very best quality.

Peel the tomatoes, remove most of the seeds and chop them finely. Make a mixture of the garlic, basil, chilli and olive oil. Mix with the tomatoes. Adjust the seasoning. Eat with pasta, and lots of Parmesan.

Zalza pikkanti

Piquant sauce

2 medium onions, chopped
4 tbsp olive oil
2 cloves garlic, chopped
Handful fresh mint and/or marjoram, chopped
3 tbsp tomato purée
1 tbsp wine vinegar
2 tsp sugar
1 tbsp black olives, stoned and chopped
1 tbsp capers
Salt and pepper

◆ Cook the onion in hot olive oil until soft and golden. Add the garlic and half the fresh herbs. Add the tomato purée. Add about 250 ml hot water. Simmer gently until thickened. Add the other ingredients, except the remaining herbs. Mix well and simmer, uncovered, for 10 minutes. Add the herbs and serve.

Zalza ħadra

Bright green parsley and garlic sauce

6 heaped tbsp fresh white bread crumbs
6 heaped tbsp fresh chopped parsley
6 large cloves garlic, chopped
1 tbsp wine vinegar
4 tbsp olive oil
Salt and pepper

◆ Mix all the ingredients together, turn into a small dish. The amount of oil and vinegar may be adjusted to taste. Float a little oil on the top at the end. Simply made and delicious with boiled beef or snails, or to accompany fresh hot potatoes or other vegetables.

Sauce Maltaise

2 egg yolks
Pinch salt
Freshly ground pepper (preferably white)
75 g butter
Grated rind and juice of a small Malta blood orange
2 tbsp cream whipped, but not too thickly

◆ This sauce is named after the sweet red orange, the Malta orange. Place the yolks, salt and pepper and 15 g of the butter in a bowl or the top of a double-boiler and mix well with a wooden spoon. Place the basin over a saucepan of simmering water and add half the orange juice; whisk until fairly thick. Add the remaining butter, cut into pieces each the size of a sugar lump. Mix well until it is smooth and thick. Add the freshly grated rind of the orange and the rest of the juice. Last of all, fold in the whipped cream. Taste and adjust the seasoning. Serve with fried or poached fish, prawns or hot vegetables.

Zalza Russa

Russian sauce

1 medium onion, chopped
25 g butter
1 tsp olive oil
2 rashers unsmoked bacon or ham, chopped
1 very small lettuce, shredded
250 ml milk
Freshly ground black pepper
Pinch of grated nutmeg
1 tbsp double cream

◆ We have adapted this unusual recipe for contemporary kitchens from *Ctieb tal Chcina*, the Maltese recipe book first published in 1908. The remaining recipes in this chapter come from, or are based on the same source.

Cook the onion until golden but not brown in the butter and oil. Add the chopped ham or bacon and after a few minutes the shredded lettuce. Cover and cook until the lettuce wilts. Add the milk and heat it, but do not boil. Season with pepper and nutmeg. Blend or process until smooth, then rub through a sieve. Serve very hot. The sieving is not essential but makes a smoother sauce. A spoonful of cream improves it even further.

Zalza għal mal-ħaxix jew l'imqarrun

Sauce to accompany vegetables or pasta

100 g fresh pork or unsmoked bacon, chopped
2 small onions, chopped
1 carrot, chopped
25 g butter
1 tbsp olive oil
Pinch of cinnamon
375 ml milk
Salt and pepper

◆ Cook the pork or bacon and the onion and carrot in the butter and oil with the cinnamon. Add the milk and simmer for about half an hour, stirring frequently. Process in the blender then sieve into a clean saucepan. Check the seasoning. Reheat gently when required and pour over the vegetables or pasta.

Zalza Vienniża
Viennese sauce

4 anchovy fillets
2 tbsp wine vinegar
4 egg yolks
100 g ground almonds

◆ Chop the anchovies finely, mix with the vinegar and squash with a fork. Beat the egg yolks and mix, a little at a time, into the ground almonds. Now add the anchovy and vinegar mixture and mix well. A good sauce to accompany grilled meat or fish.

Zalza għal-pullam
Sauce to accompany poultry

250 ml wine vinegar
Stick of cinnamon
1 onion stuck with 3 cloves
4 slices of lemon
1 tsp of sugar
2 egg yolks, beaten

◆ Mix the first five ingredients together in a saucepan and bring to a boil, then simmer until slightly reduced. Strain through a sieve on to the beaten egg yolks, stirring all the time. Pour over the meat.

Zalza għal-laħam tal-vitella
Sauce to accompany roast veal

2 egg yolks
Juice of 1 large lemon
2 tsp caster sugar

◆ In a double-boiler or bain-marie, mix the yolks, lemon juice and sugar. Slowly add about 250 ml of the juices from the roasted meat, from which the fat has been removed. Stir until thickened. This recipe could be used with any roast joint. The sauce should not boil.

Zalza tal-Kardinal
The Cardinal's sauce

Juice and pulp of 1 large or 2 small lemons
2 tsp zest of lemon
25 g parsley
2 cloves garlic
1 tsp wine vinegar
1–2 tbsp olive oil
Salt
Cayenne pepper
Sugar

◆ Combine all the ingredients save the olive oil in a blender. Process. Add the olive oil gradually, processing again. Check for sale, cayenne and sugar. This sauce goes well with grilled fish and vegetables. The author of *Ctieb tal Chcina* recommends sieving it but we don't think this is essential. If you are without a blender, all the ingredients can be chopped, then pounded in a mortar. before adding the olive oil.

Zalza alla Byron
Lord Byron's sauce

2 tender celery hearts
2 tbsp parsley
Capers, garlic and fresh marjoram to taste
3 hard-boiled egg yolks
2 tbsp olive oil
1 tbsp wine vinegar
Salt and pepper
Mustard powder

◆ This is another 'raw' sauce from the author of *Ctieb tal Chcina*. She suggests the reader pounds the celery, parsley, garlic, marjoram and capers in a pestle and mortar. Today, the effect can be attained using a blender or processor. Mix in the egg yolks, olive oil and vinegar. Add salt, pepper and mustard powder to taste. You might like to add a half teaspoon of caster sugar.

Zalza tal-inċova alla ġinevrina

Anchovy sauce

1 small onion, chopped
2 cloves garlic, crushed
2 rashers bacon or fresh pork, finely chopped
2 tsp butter
1 tsp olive oil
2 tsp flour
125 ml chicken stock
4–6 anchovy fillets, chopped
1 tbsp capers, chopped

◆ Cook the chopped onion, garlic and bacon in the butter and oil until they are golden and the onion is soft. Stir in the flour, then gradually add the stock. Bring slowly to the boil and simmer on low heat for 5 minutes. Add the anchovies and press through a sieve. Add the capers. Serve with grilled meat or chicken.

Zalza tad-dar

An everyday household sauce

2 tsp butter
1 tsp olive oil
2 tsp plain flour
2 onions, chopped
2 carrots, chopped
2 cloves of garlic, chopped
1 tbsp celery, chopped
4 cloves
2 bay leaves
2 tsp marjoram, chopped
250 ml red wine
1 tbsp wine vinegar
Salt and pepper

◆ Melt the butter, add the olive oil and fry gently all the vegetables until soft and turning golden. Mix in the flour and add the herbs, cloves, salt and pepper. Add the wine, vinegar, and an equivalent quantity of water. Simmer for 20 minutes. Process to a purée in a blender, sieve (if desired) and serve hot with roast pork or chops.

Zalza tas-serva
The maid's sauce

2 egg yolks
125 ml chicken or beef stock
2 tbsp parsley, chopped
Salt and pepper
Lemon juice

◆ Beat the egg yolks in a basin set over simmering water, or the top half of a double boiler, and gradually whisk in the hot stock. Add the parsley and seasoning. Allow to thicken, stirring all the time. A sauce like this should not be boiled. Just before serving, add lemon juice to taste and serve hot with grilled meat or fish or with vegetables.

Zalza Cesare Borgia
Cesare Borgia sauce

½ bottle of red wine
2 cloves garlic
6 sage leaves
1 slice toast, broken into pieces
1–2 tbsp olive oil

◆ Heat the wine with all the other ingredients, bring to the boil, then simmer for a few minutes. Strain through a fine sieve. Reheat before serving, reducing by boiling, if necessary, to a suitable consistency. This is to accompany game or grilled meat.

Mayonnaise

◆ Bottles of commercially manufactured mayonnaise of varied quality can be found at every supermarket. Some are acceptable (especially the more expensive, French, brands) but many are to be avoided at all costs – just read the list of ingredients! Food processors and blenders make it only too easy to make your own mayonnaise, provided you choose the best ingredients (fresh egg yolks, in preference to the whole egg, virgin olive oil, fresh lemon juice or a little white wine vinegar, perhaps tarragon flavoured for certain dishes.) The day might come when you won't have access to machines so it is as well to know how to make mayonnaise using a bowl and spoon and human energy. We were taught by Duminka Farrugia many years ago. It is a lesson you never forget! Sit comfortably, wear an apron and have a small bowl held between your knees. Use a silver or stainless steel teaspoon to start with. Stir two fresh egg yolks, very vigorously and add not more than two drops of olive oil and stir them in very thoroughly. Repeat this process very patiently until the bulk of egg yolk and oil has doubled. Now you can increase the amount of oil you add but always beat in well after each addition, increasing gradually to a teaspoon at a time and when the mixture has trebled you increase the quantity of oil still further. Continue in this way until you have the quantity you want – the mixture should be glistening and fairly thick, like an ointment. Now stir in a little lemon juice or white wine vinegar, to taste and season with salt and a little white pepper. Mayonnaise should not taste sharp and very vinegary. **Note:** If you are making a mayonnaise to accompany shellfish and you want to give it a hot peppery flavour you can substitute sunflower or groundnut oil for some of the olive oil. For other dishes you can turn it into an aioli by adding plenty of crushed garlic.

Saving a curdled mayonnaise

◆ If your mayonnaise begins to separate while you are making it, try to save it, as quickly as possibly by whisking in a teaspoon or two of boiling water – depending on the quantity you have at the time. Stir furiously for a few minutes. If this trick works resume the addition of olive oil very carefully. If it does not you need to start all over again with another egg yolk, adding the curdled mixture drop by drop, then proceed with the olive oil as before. Practice definitely makes perfect. Some chefs add a teaspoon of boiling water at the end to improve the keeping qualities. Others heat the vinegar. We have not tried this.

Zalza ħafifa tal-ħjar u tursin

Light Cucumber and Parsley Sauce

A large handful of fresh parsley;
2 to 3 slices of white bread
1 small cucumber
3 to 4 tablespoons very good virgin olive oil
Juice of a large lemon
2 to 3 cloves fresh garlic
Salt and freshly ground pepper

◆ This is a recipe we have devised from various sources and experiments – it is as creamy and delicious as mayonnaise, much lighter and goes well with many fish dishes.

You will need a liquidiser for this. First place the parsley and garlic in the liquidiser and chop. Now add the peeled and chopped cucumber and the bread, (with crusts removed) soaked briefly in cold water and squeezed out. Add the lemon juice the seasoning and the olive oil. Blend till smooth and chill until ready to use. If too thick you can add a small amount of cold water and blend again.

Zalza Bechamel

Bechamel sauce

250 mls (half a pint) milk
20 g (.75 of an ounce) each butter and plain flour
A slice of onion (optional)
a bay leaf
Freshly grated nutmeg
salt and freshly ground black white pepper

◆ This famous French sauce is popular in the cuisines of all western nations – it is an excellent sauce if properly made and there are countless variations which can be found in many recipe books. One needs to think in terms of ratios – the basic ingredients are the same, but one varies the ratio of butter and flour to milk according to how the sauce is to be used. The standard recipe is for 25g each of butter and flour to 250 mls milk but if your recipe requires a thinner sauce (e.g. to pour over fish) then the amount of milk or other liquid is increased. The following ingredients make a not too thick bechamel sauce, suitable for lasagne for example.

Heat the milk very gently with the spices, onion and bay leaf. Cover and leave to infuse for ten to 15 minutes. Strain. Melt the butter over low heat, add the flour and mix well. Slowly add about a third of the milk and blend it in stirring all the time. Slowly add the remainder of the milk. Bring to a boil and keep stirring, then leave to simmer (preferably on a metal mat) over very low heat for a further 10 minutes. This simmering is crucial. If you stop cooking the sauce as soon as it has thickened you get a very floury taste. **Note:** this is a much easier method which produces an equally good result. After infusing the spices and straining the milk, place the butter and flour in your blender, pour on the milk and blend on fast speed until you have a smooth mixture (a few seconds). Return this mixture to the pan and stir over low heat until the mixture comes to a boil, then simmer as before.

BIBLIOGRAPHY

Ananda Marga Centre, Malta, *What's Wrong with Eating Meat?* (n.d.).

Arberry, A. J., 'A Baghdad Cookery Book', *Islamic Culture*, No.13., 1939.

Badger, G.P., *Description of Malta and Gozo*, M. Weiss, Malta (1838).

Barbara, J., *Ismijet tar-Ħut tal-Mediterran*, Dipartiment tal-Agrikoltura u Sajd, Malta (1976).

Bini, G. (ed.), *Catalogue of Names of Fish, Molluscs and Crustaceans of Commercial Importance in the Mediterranean*, FAO, Milan (1965).

Boni, A., *Il Talismano delta Felicità*, 19th edition, Carlo Colombo, Rome.

Brydone, P., FRS, *A Tour of Sicily and Malta, in a Series of Letters to William Beckford, Esq., of Somerly in Suffolk*, London (1773).

Buttigieg, Joseph, *A New Approach to Maltese Gardening*, privately published, Malta (1987).

Carbonaro, Carmen, *Recipes of Maltese Dishes*, Giovanni Muscat, Malta (1969).

Capra, Fritjof, Steindl-Rast, David and Matus, Thomas. Belonging to the Universe – New Thinking About God and Nature, Penguin, London 1992.

Caruana, A.A., *Molluscorum Gaulo-Melitensium of the late Guiseppe Mamo*, British Press, Malta (1867).

Caruana, P. *Siġar tal-Frott*, privately published, Malta (n.d.).

Cassar, C., *Fenkata: An Emblem of Maltese Peasant Resistance*, Ministry for Youth and the Arts, Malta (1994).

Cavaliero, Roderick. The Last of the Crusaders, Penguin, London 1994.

Chatto, J. and Martin, W.I., *A Kitchen in Corfu*, Chatto & Windus, London (1993).

Chiron, H., *Il-Ħobż Malti – is Sengħa tal-Furnar*, Medigrain Ltd., Malta (1994).

Davenport, R., *Sourdough Cookery*, Bantam Books in association with H.P. Books, Arizona (1977).

David, Elizabeth, *English Bread and Yeast Cookery*, Penguin, Harmondsworth (1977).

—*French Provincial Cooking*, Michael Joseph, London (1960).

—*An Omelette and a Glass of Wine*, Robert Hale, A Jill Norman Book, London (1984).

—*Italian Food*, Penguin, Harmondsworth (1954)

Davidson, Alan, *Mediterranean Seafood*, Penguin, Harmondsworth (2nd ed. 1981).

—*The Tio Pepe Guide to the Seafood of Spain and Portugal*, Gonzales Byass, Jerez (1992).

F.A.O., *Species Identification Sheets for the Mediterranean and the Black Sea*, Rome (1987).

Goode, J. and Wilson, C., *Fruit and Vegetables of the World*, Lothian, Australia (1987).

Kininmonth, Christopher, *Travellers' Guide to Malta and Gozo*, Cape, London (1967).

Jones, Steve, The Language of the Genes, Penguin, London 1994.

Lanfranco, Guido G., *The Fish Around Malta* Progress Press Ltd., Malta (1993).

Luke, Sir Harry, *Malta An Account and an Appreciation*, Harrap, London (1949).

—*The Tenth Muse*, Putnam, London (1954).

Martin, Ruth, *International Dictionary of Food and Cooking*, Constable, London (1973).

Monson, W.I., *Journal*, Rodwell and Martin, London (1820),

Moore Lappé, Frances, *Diet for a Small Planet,* Ballantine Books, New York (1971).

Oxford Book of Plants. Oxford University Press, Oxford 1969.

Parkinson-Large, Pamela, *A Taste of History: The Food of the Knights of Malta*, Melitensia Art Gallery, Malta (1995).

Poilâne, Lionel, *Guide de l'Amateur du Pain*, Paris (1981).

Roden, Claudia, *A Book of Middle Eastern Food*, Penguin, Harmondsworth. (1976).

Schemerhorn, Elizabeth, *Malta of the Knights*, Heinemann, London (1929).

Scurfield, George and Cecilia, *Home Baked*, Faber and Faber, London (1956).

Simeti, Mary Taylor, *Sicilian Food*, Century, London (1989).

Stobart, T. The Cook's Encyclopaedia, Papermac, London 1982.

Stubbs, Joyce M., *The Home Book of Greek Cookery*, Faber and Faber, London (1963).

Vella, E.L.V., *Ctieb tal Chcina*, A.C. Aquilina & Co, Malta (1908).

Vella, Marie, *Cooking the Maltese Way*, Cordina's Emporium, Malta (n.d., 2nd ed.).

Wilson, C. Anne, *The Book of Marmalade*, Constable, London (1985).

Zeldin, Theodore. An Intimate History of Humanity,, Sinclair-Stevenson, London 1994.

INDEX